Freshwater Fishing Tips and Techniques

Gene Kugach

STACKPOLE
BOOKS

Published by
STACKPOLE BOOKS
5067 Ritter Road
Mechanicsburg, PA 17055

Printed in the United States of America

10 9 8 7 6 5 4 3 2

First edition

Library of Congress Cataloging-in-Publication Data

Kugach, Gene.
    Freshwater fishing tips and techniques / Gene Kugach.
        p.   cm.
    ISBN 0-8117-2765-3 (pb)
    1. Fishing.   2. Freshwater fishes.   I. Title.
SH441.K84 1997
799.1'1—dc20

96-27885
CIP

*To my wife, Bernadette, my daughter, Michelle,
and my grandchildren,
Lauren Ann and Kristen Ashley*

Contents

5 Fly Fishing

6 Fly Tying

7 Ice Fishing

8 Tackle

PREFACE

This is my second book on the subject of fishing. As in the first book, I tried to illustrate as much of the subject matter as possible to make it more meaningful and understandable.

Much of the information contained in this book has been around for a number of years, in one form or another, and has proven to be useful to many fishermen.

I hope my efforts in collecting and compiling all of the information presented here help the reader to be more successful in his or her fishing endeavors.

Gene Kugach

ACKNOWLEDGMENTS

Books and Pamphlets:
Fly Tying, John F. McKim
Complete Fly Tying Instruction Book, Hobby Bait Industries
Practical Flies and Their Construction, Gee and Sias
Publications by the Illinois Department of Conservation.

Magazines:
Mid West Outdoors, Outdoor Notebook, The In Fisherman,
Fishing Facts, Sports Afield, Great Lakes Fisherman,
Salmon/Trout/Steelheader, Fly Fisherman, Rod and Reel,
Fishing World, and Fins and Feathers.

Manufacturers' Catalogs:
Shakespeare, Eagle Claw, Mustad, South Bend, Orvis, Tackle-Craft,
Trilene, Cortland, Grizzly Inc., Mister Twister, Northland Tackle Co.,
Lindy-Little Joe Inc., and Du Pont Stren.

CHAPTER
1
GENERAL FISHING TIPS

General Fishing

Most anglers who are successful and who are considered lucky are really educated anglers who utilize experience and knowledge.

Fishing success can be obtained only by understanding and applying basic fishing knowledge rather than depending on luck alone.

Much of the information contained in this chapter has been compiled from experience obtained during many hours of fishing, and input and feedback from other successful anglers.

The following pages include information that can make a big difference in filling a stringer full of fish, or going home empty-handed.

Included are many tricks, tips, and suggestions on how to improve your fishing skills, how to locate fish, as well as some common sense tips on ways to make your fishing experience more enjoyable.

I hope that some of the information presented here will improve your skills and help you catch more fish.

FISHING ETHICS

The following are a few simple things to remember to make fishing a more enjoyable sport for everyone.

- Keep only the fish you can use.
- Practice "Catch and Release."
- Don't be a polluter. Properly dispose of your trash (tangled line, bait containers, and so forth).
- Observe angling and boating regulations.
- Respect other fishermen's rights
- Respect property owners' rights.
- Support local conversation efforts.
- Never release fish, baits, or plants into public waters.
- Share your knowledge and skills with other anglers.
- Promote the sport of fishing.

TEN COMMON FISHING MISTAKES

You probably will catch more fish if you avoid making the following mistakes.

1. USING OLD LINE
   Solution: Replace or change your line frequently.

2. USING DIRTY OR FAULTY REELS
   Solution: Keep your equipment clean and in good working order

3. IMPROPERLY SETTING YOUR DRAG
   Solution: Adjust and set your drag before you start fishing.

4. USING DULL HOOKS
   Solution: Make sure your hooks are sharp.

5. USING ONLY YOUR FAVORITE LURE
   Solution: Try different lures, colors, sizes, shapes. "EXPERIMENT."

6. FISHING ONLY ONE LOCATION
   Solution: Try new areas.

7. FISHING FOR ONLY ONE SPECIES
   Solution: Be versatile.

8. BEING UNOBSERVANT
   Solution: Observe conditions, weather, temperature, and so forth.

9. LACKING CONCENTRATION
   Solution: Concentrate on catching one fish at a time.

10. LACKING CONFIDENCE
   Solution: Have a positive mental attitude.

KEEPING A FISHING LOG

To improve your future results, try the following suggestions before you plan your next fishing trip.

■ Start keeping records (Fishing Log) of the waters you have fished in the past.

■ Record the fish you caught, the time of day when you caught them, the season, the weather conditions, and the bait or lures you used.

■ Also get a map or make one of the lake you're fishing and mark the locations that were productive.

By studying your notes, you can key in on the areas that proved to be productive and improve your chances for a successful trip.

BASIC FISHING LOG SUGGESTIONS

The following are a list of things to consider including in a fishing log.

■ **Body of Water**
Name: Lake, River, Stream, Pond

■ **Time of Year**
Season: Spring, Summer, Fall, Winter
Month: Date, Time of day

■ **Weather Conditions**
Air Temperature: Hot, Cool, Cold, Average
Wind: Speed, Direction
Sky: Clear, Overcast, Rainy, Stormy
Barometer: Steady, Rising, Falling

■ **Water Conditions**
Clarity: Clear, Muddy, Stained
Temperature: Warm, Cool, Cold
Water Level: High, low, normal

■ **Bait Used**
Live: Type, Size
Lures: Type, Size, Color

■ **Presentation**
Depth: Deep, Shallow, No. of feet
Retrieve: Slow, Fast, Medium

■ **Location**
Where Caught: Reference Points, Type of structure,Open Water, Shoreline,

■ **Fish Caught**
Species: Number, Size, Weight

■ **Remarks**
General Thoughts

In addition to the above list of suggestions, you can also add anything that you feel will be of future value.

FISHING LOG

BODY OF WATER:
❑ Lake ❑ River ❑ Stream ❑ Creek ❑ Pond ❑ Quarry ❑ Reservoir

NAME:_____

LOCATION:_____

DATE:_____

TIME OF YEAR:
❑ Spring ❑ Summer ❑ Fall ❑ Winter

TIME OF DAY:
❑ Morning ❑ Midday ❑ Evening ❑ Night
Time Started_____Time Finished_____

WEATHER CONDITIONS:
Sky: ❑ Clear/Sunny ❑ Overcast ❑ Partly Cloudy ❑ Fog
Precipitation: ❑ Rainy ❑ Drizzle ❑ Storms ❑ Snow
Variables: ❑ Cold Front Approaching ❑ Cold Front Leaving
Barometer: ❑ Steady ❑ Rising ❑ Falling
Moon Phase: ❑ New ❑ Full ❑ Waning ❑ Waxing
Air Temperature: ❑ Hot ❑ Cold ❑ Cool ❑ Average
Wind Conditions: ❑ Strong ❑ Moderate ❑ Light ❑None
Wind Direction: ❑N ❑S ❑E ❑W ❑NE ❑NW ❑SE ❑SW

WATER CONDITIONS:
Clarity: ❑ Dirty ❑ Stained ❑ Clear ❑ Muddy
Current: ❑ Fast ❑ Moderate ❑ Slow ❑ None
Water Level: ❑ Normal ❑ High ❑ Low
Surface Conditions: ❑ Rough ❑ Choppy ❑ Calm ❑ Slight Ripple

FISHING TECHNIQUE:
❑ Boat Fishing ❑ Shore Fishing
❑ Spinning ❑ Bait Casting ❑ Still Fishing ❑ Fly Fishing
❑ Trolling ❑ Ice Fishing ❑ Other

REMARKS:_____
_____
_____
_____
_____
_____

FISHING LOG*

GENERAL INFORMATION	SPECIES*				
	Fish #1	Fish #2	Fish #3	Fish #4	Fish #5
Time Caught					
Length					
Girth					
Weight					
METHOD USED					
Spinning					
Bait Casting					
Still Fishing					
Trolling					
Fly Fishing					
BAIT USED					
Lure Type					
Color					
Size					
Live Bait (Type)					
Live Bait (Size)					
Depth Caught (Ft.)					
PRESENTATION					
Slow Retrieve					
Fast Retrieve					
Med. Retrieve					
LOCATION:					
Map Ref. Points					
STRUCTURE					
Weeds					
Gravel					
Lily Pads					
Pier/Dock					
Rocks					
Open Water					
Tree Stumps					
Other					

* New sheet required for each species caught.

6

WEATHER TIPS

COMMON SENSE TIPS

Here are some simple things to remember regarding weather to make your fishing trips more enjoyable and safer.

■ Be aware of weather changes and how fast they occur. Rapid shifts in wind direction can mean foul weather is approaching.

■ Check the weather report before going out on a lake, especially a large lake.

■ On large bodies of water, have a compass, a radio tuned to a weather channel, lake charts, and running lights on your boat. Wind changes, storms, and fog can occur quickly.

■ Never fish during a lightning storm.

WIND THEORY
(Author unknown)

Here's an old theory that's been around for years about the wind and its effect on fishing.

Wind from the **north**, fisherman does not go forth.
Wind from the **south**, blows the bait in the fish's mouth.
Wind from the **east**, the fish bite least.
Wind from the **west**, the fish bite best.

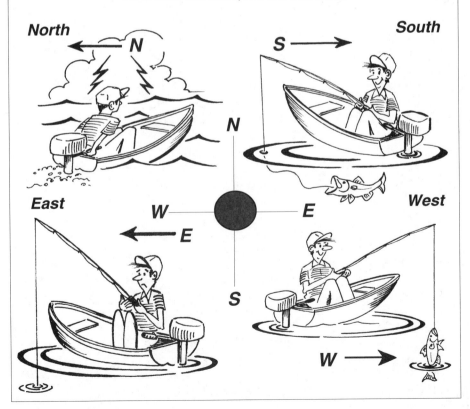

BAROMETRIC CONDITIONS

Barometers are used to foretell changes in the weather. Falling barometric preasure indicates an approaching storm or a major weather change such as a cold front, while a rising or steady barometer can mean pleasant conditions.

Barometric pressures also affect fish, some more than others. With fish, a falling barometer usually precedes exceptionally poor fishing, while a steady slowly rising barometer will produce the best fishing. However, many fishermen figure that it matters little if a barometer is low or high, as long as it is steady.

The following information regarding what the weather conditions will be by the fall or rise of a barometer is a rule of thumb. Conditions can vary by geographical locations and other unpredictable factors.

Falling Barometer

Barometer Reading	Possible Weather Conditions
31 to 30.8	Fair, cool, variable winds
30.8 to 30.5	Fair, warmer, windy, changing to rain
30.5 to 30.2	Developing storms
30.2 to 29.9	Warmer and cloudy, possible rain.
29.9 to 29.6	Warmer, increasing winds, unsettled weather
29.6 to 29.3	Clearing, warming trend
29.3 to 29.0	Clearing, windy, and cooler weather
29.0 to 28.7	Storms

Rising Barometer

Barometer Reading	Possible Weather Conditions
29.0 to 29.3	Clearing, cool, high winds
29.3 to 29.6	Cool, high winds, possible rain
29.6 to 29.9	Fair, windy
29.9 to 30.2	Fair, windy with diminishing winds
30.2 to 30.5	Fair, cool, variable winds
30.5 to 30.8	Clear, cool, moderate winds
30.8 to 31.0	Rain, high winds

WEATHER CONDITIONS

Weather conditions can be the difference between a full stringer or practice casting. It affects all fish (some more than others) and their habits. Most experienced fishermen know the importance of recognizing various conditions (barometric pressures, overcast skies, temperature changes, seasonal changes, winds, and so forth) and adapting their fishing skills to successfully overcome these differences. The following are a few helpfull tips regarding weather conditions.

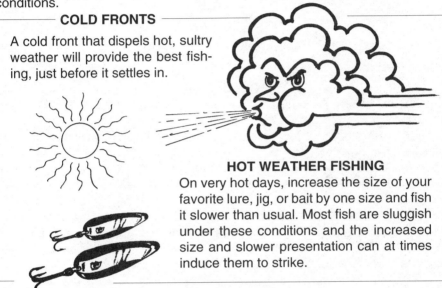

COLD FRONTS

A cold front that dispels hot, sultry weather will provide the best fishing, just before it settles in.

HOT WEATHER FISHING

On very hot days, increase the size of your favorite lure, jig, or bait by one size and fish it slower than usual. Most fish are sluggish under these conditions and the increased size and slower presentation can at times induce them to strike.

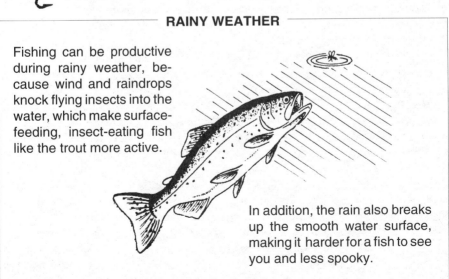

RAINY WEATHER

Fishing can be productive during rainy weather, because wind and raindrops knock flying insects into the water, which make surface-feeding, insect-eating fish like the trout more active.

In addition, the rain also breaks up the smooth water surface, making it harder for a fish to see you and less spooky.

POND FISHING TIPS

POND FISHING

Thousands of farm ponds, small lakes, and community ponds/lakes are scattered throughout the United States.

These small bodies of water afford many fishermen an opportunity for some excellent fishing during any season.

During the winter months most ice fishermen will have the advantage of fishing early, because these small ponds or lakes freeze up much earlier than most larger lakes.

During early spring, they warm much more quickly than larger lakes, and the warmer water temperatures induce spawning about a month earlier for most freshwater fish. These conditions after a long winter give the fisherman with cabin fever an opportunity to get a jump on the season.

During the summer and fall months, fishing will also be good, due to the lack of fishing pressure, unlike that found on larger lakes.

The following are just a few suggestions on how to locate and fish some of the local ponds found in your area.

■ To find your local ponds, contact your local county office and request a detailed county road map. These maps will indicate pond locations as well as access roads to reach them.

■ For other than your own local county, contact your State Geological Survey Department or the U.S. Geological Survey Department and request topographical maps of the areas you are interested in. In most cases, maps of the requested areas will be available and will be sent to you for a nominal fee.

Once you receive the maps, select a few likely ponds in a given area and talk to the various owners. It's important to get permission from the owners to fish their ponds. Don't, I repeat, don't trespass without permission.

In most situations, if you present yourself properly, abide by the owner's rules, and treat his property with respect, permission will be granted. Sometimes it may require a small fee to be paid, or perhaps a few of the fish you catch, to gain access, but in the long run, it's well worth it.

STRIP MINE OR QUARRY FISHING TIPS

Strip mines or quarry lakes can be tough lakes to fish, but like any tough lake, if you use common sense and observe various conditions (water temperature, season, water clarity, cover and so forth), you can have successful results by applying some basic considerations.

TYPES OF QUARRY/STRIP MINE LAKES

Category 1: A large, long (quarter mile or more) narrow, deep pit with a steep shoreline, breaking sharply to deep water.

Category 2: Usually half the size and depth of a category one lake, with a more convoluted irregular shoreline that has a large amount of weed growth and shallow flats.

Category 3: A dishpan or pothole lake, which characteristically is ten to fifteen feet deep and has a shoreline that is covered with emergent vegetation and surrounded with cattails.

CONSIDERATIONS

1. In the spring, when the water temperature reaches 50 degrees, fish the smaller lakes (categories two and three) and the shallowest water available.

2. From spring to summer, as the water warms, work the edges that have access to deeper water.

3. Midsummer, avoid working waters that are over fifteen feet deep. The deeper waters stratify and are devoid of oxygen.

4. When the fall turnover begins, switch to larger pits (category one or two). Bass are less likely to be scattered in larger lakes, more so than in the smaller lakes (category three).

5. Regardless of the season, use a light line and live bait presentation; most fish will be extremely sight oriented in their feeding habits due to the water clarity.

6. Use polaroid sunglasses. Because of the water clarity, you will be able to spot cruising fish or potential structure.

BEST STRIP MINE OR QUARRY RIG
AND HOW TO USE IT

The following rig and its use is directed toward bass fishing, but it is also effective for most other species found in a typical strip mine or quarry lake.

RIGGING

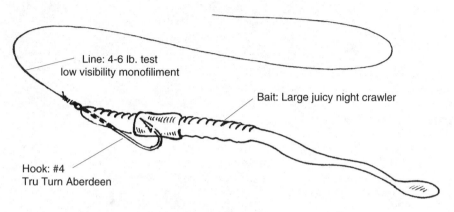

Line: 4-6 lb. test
low visibility monofiliment

Bait: Large juicy night crawler

Hook: #4
Tru Turn Aberdeen

PRESENTATION

Attach the night crawler as shown above, without using any additional weights. After you cast the bait, allow it to sink naturally in a slow semi-suspended manor. Once it hits bottom, let it sit for a while (thirty or sixty seconds) before starting your retrieve. In clear or sandy bottom areas, allow it to sit as much as three to four minutes. If the bottom is heavily weeded or moss covered, retrieve and cast to a new location. While the bait is sinking or on the bottom, keep your reel bail open (free line) and use your finger against the line to detect any strikes. When you get a strike, let the fish take line for five to ten seconds before setting the hook.

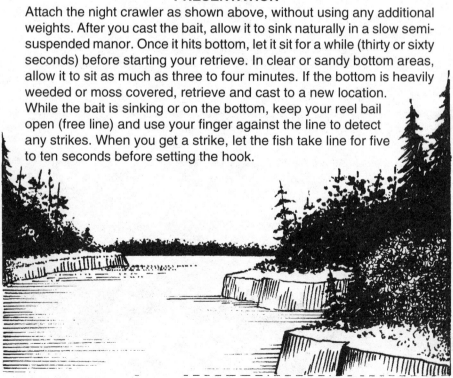

STRIP MINE OR QUARRY FISHING TIPS

The following are just a few major points to consider when strip mine or quarry lake fishing.

GENERAL FISHING TIPS

■ The banks of strip mines fall off quickly into deep water. Fish parallel to the shore and try different depths with your presentations until you find the fish.

■ Use lighter line due to the water clarity, and light-colored lures for low light conditions.

■ In the spring, jig and pig combinations are effective in black, brown, or black/blue color selections. Also effective are spinnerbaits in white or white/chartreuse or crankbaits in crawdad or chrome colors.

■ In the summer, plastic worms 4-6 inches long rigged Carolina style or deep running crankbaits in bluegill or chrome colors are effective. You can also have some good results using topwater buzzbaits.

■ In the fall, stay with the typical summer baits, switching to the spring combinations in the late fall.

WATER CLARITY

Strip mine/quarry water clarity is due to the following factors.

■ They are small bodies of water with steep banks that protect them from wind effects.

■ They have bottoms that are made up of sand, shale, slate, and gravel, which keep the water clear even after a heavy rain.

■ They are not fed by any feeder creeks as in the case of reservoirs or ponds which add sediment after rainstorms.

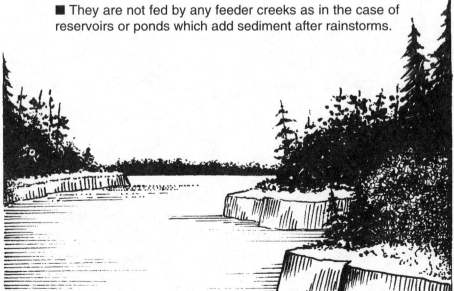

RIVER FISHING

Most rivers are full of snags, hang-ups, and fast-moving currents, which cause a lot of tackle loss for most fishermen. To cut down on your losses, try some of the following tips and techniques.

■ **Line:** Starting with the line, unless you're fishing for giant-sized catfish, use lighter line. The heavier the line, the more weight required for casting as well as keeping the bait on the bottom. Switch to a six- to eight-pound test line, which in most cases will be adequate for most species of fish.

■ **Hooks:** Don't use double, treble, or heavy tempered steel hooks. These types of hooks catch and hold snags and rocks very easily and are difficult to dislodge. The proper hook to use should be a light wire, non-tempered type that sets easily in the fish's mouth, and if it snags, or gets hung up, will pull out or bend without breaking your line.

■ **Weights:** Don't use fat, heavy weights, because they offer more resistance to the water and will snag more easily. Use a dropper line with small removable "BB" type split shots to keep the bait down. Only use enough weight to have the bait touch bottom, allowing it to move with the current. The dropper rig may need adjustment by adding or removing some of the split shots, depending on the depth and water current.

Below are various examples of how to set up your rig.

BASIC RIVER RIGS

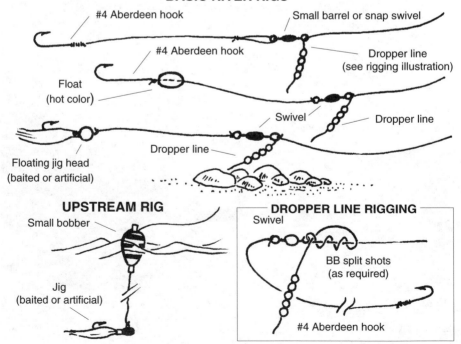

#4 Aberdeen hook

Small barrel or snap swivel

#4 Aberdeen hook

Dropper line
(see rigging illustration)

Float
(hot color)

Swivel

Dropper line

Floating jig head
(baited or artificial)

Dropper line

UPSTREAM RIG

Small bobber

Jig
(baited or artificial)

DROPPER LINE RIGGING

Swivel

BB split shots
(as required)

#4 Aberdeen hook

CROSS CURRENT FISHING

Cross current is one of the best methods to river fish, it allows you to cover a greater area where fish may be holding. To properly fish cross current, try the following:

1. Use a dropper rig with the minimum amount of weight necessary to touch bottom with your bait.

2. Cast slightly upstream toward the river bank, allowing the current to carry the bait directly downstream.

3. Vary the distance of each cast to cover a greater area.

4. Vary the point where you retrieve your bait.

5. Repeat two through three, until you completely covered the area you are fishing.

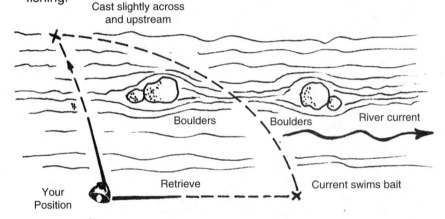

UPSTREAM FISHING

The advantages of upstream fishing is as follows.

■ Most fish face upstream in their holding areas, waiting for food to come down with the current.

■ There is less chance of spooking the fish because they can't see you.

To properly fish upstream, try the following:

1. Cast beyond the area where you believe fish are holding, letting your presentation sink, and allowing the current to carry it to the spot you want to reach.

2. Use a small float as a strike indicator and to keep your presentation just off the bottom.

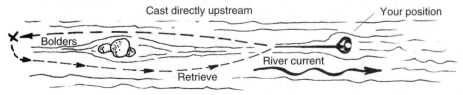

DOWNSTREAM FISHING

Downstream fishing is the least favored method to river fish. The reasons are as follows:

- The bait or lure will disturb the fish holding areas directly below you.
- Heavier current will require more weight to sink your rig.
- Additional weight will add to the risk of more hang-ups.

To properly fish downstream, try the following:

1. Basic Rig: Tie on a small barrel swivel to the end of your line (8 lb. test), with a dropper rig for your weights (BB split shots), which should only be heavy enough to keep the bait down. Add your hook (#4 Aberdeen) or your lure to the opposite end of the swivel.

2. Cast the rig slightly across and downstream, keeping your rod tip low, allowing the current to swim the bait or lure across deeper water.

3. Raise the rod tip higher when you encounter shallower water to keep the bait or lure up and over any snags.

4. When the bait or lure is directly downstream, retrieve it slowly and repeat two through three until you cover the area you are fishing.

Cast slightly across
and downstream

Boulders

Current swims bait

River current

Boulders

Retrieve

Your
position

16

RIVER FISHING TIPS

SHORELINE RIVER FISHING

When river waters fluctuate, shore fisherman can use these conditions to their advantage.

Fishing near highway or railroad trestles during an increase of water flow is a good way to filll a stringer.

Good-sized eddies are formed by the abutments favoring the bank sides, which are excellent fish hold-ing locations.

Other good areas to try are the dikes or spillways on larger rivers.

Check the spillways where the faster water flows enter; there will be a distinct current edge where fish like to hold. Also fish above the spillway where the water flows over it; white bass like to hold right above the edge and feed on minnows and insects before they are swept over the top.

FALL RIVER FISHING

The advantage of fall river fishing is the un-crowded waters. During the month of Octo-ber, most fishermen are busy hunting or wait-ing for ice fishing to start, eliminating a lot of the competition for productive fishing areas along the river.

During this time of the fall season, fish like the walleye will be located in the same areas that they are found in during the spring season. Bass will drop out of feeder creeks and streams into the main river channel. Pike will be found in the backwater sloughs, along the edges of weeds that are still green, but in deeper water than during the summer months. Most any species found in the river at this time will still be active.

As the river waters cool and the temperatures drop, so should the speed of your presentation. The key to successful fall fishing is your presentation. No longer can you just cast and speed crank, you must switch to a slower lift and drop or steady slow swimming retrieve to make your presentation more effective.

Other than your favorite lure or baits, try some jigs tipped with minnows or twister tails for the walleyes or bass, or a golden shiner on a bobber rig for the northerns.

Without a doubt, a slower presentation during this time of year will produce some of the finest fishing of any season.

LOCATING FISH

One of the keys to successful fishing is the ability to locate the fish. The following are just a few examples of what to look for when you're out on a river, stream, pond or lake, which may make your search a little easier.

SPRING FED LAKES

Springs found in many lakes are excellent areas for locating fish. To locate springs, especially during the summer, watch the early morning mists. The mist that remains after most mist has evaporated from the water surface in other areas will indicate the springs location.

LOCATING SPRINGS

Try this if you own or can rent a aluminum boat on a spring fed lake.Take off your shoes and socks and go exploring barefoot in your boat. When your feet start getting cold, you have found the spring.

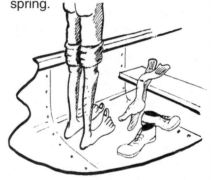

BIRD WATCHING

If you see a flock of feeding gulls hovering near the water's surface, chances are they are feeding on bait fish, which will also attract game fish. Don't pass up the area; try some cast into or as close as possible to the spot where the gulls are. Try some small live minnows or minnow-imitating lures such as streamer flies with a lot of flash.

FOAM PATCHES

Don't overlook the patches of foam that collect around submerged rocks or fallen trees. Food collects in these areas on the upstream side and attracts feeding fish. Cast your presentation twenty to thirty feet above the area and allow the current to carry it in.

Foam

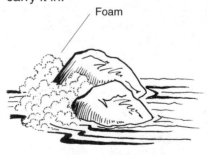

FISH ATTRACTOR

Here's an old trick that will improve your fishing most any time of the day or season. All you need is an empty two-liter pop bottle, a piece of cord, and a few live minnows out of your bait bucket. Here's what you do.

ASSEMBLY

Step 1

Starting with the empty two-liter pop bottle, place the bottle into some hot water for a few minutes until the glue that holds the black base and the label in place softens. Remove the base with a twisting motion, and peel off the label.

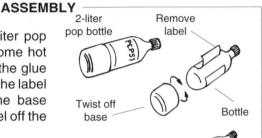

2-liter pop bottle

Remove label

Twist off base

Bottle

Step 2

Next, using a hot nail or a drill, burn or drill a dozen or more holes into the sides and bottom of the bottle and a few more holes around the bottle neck.

Burn or drill holes

Step 3

Next burn or drill a hole in the center of the bottle cap large enough to insert the cord and tie the cord to a small nail, washer, or anything small enough to fit into the inside of the cap. Screw the cap back onto the bottle and your attractor rig is ready to use.

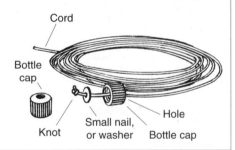

Cord

Bottle cap

Knot

Small nail, or washer

Hole

Bottle cap

HOW IT WORKS

After you have your bait and you're out on the water, fill the bottle with water by immersing it into your minnow bucket or along the side of the boat. Put about a dozen small minnows into the bottle and screw the cap onto the bottle.

Using the cord, lower the bottle and the minnows to the depth you're planning to fish and secure it to the boat. Lower your baited rig as close to the bottle as possible and watch out. The minnows in the bottle are like a magnet for attracting perch, crappies, or most any species of fish.

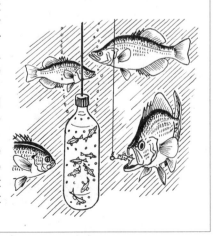

FISH ATTRACTORS

Anyone who fishes extensively knows the value of using fish attractors to improve their catching ability. Attractors such as scented oils, flashers, chum, and so forth have worked over the years and are now offered by many manufacturers and are currently available in most tackle shops. The following are just a few tips on using attractors which may be useful to try the next time you go fishing.

SCENT ATTRACTION

If you're a live bait fisherman, here's a tip to try with your artificial plastic or rubber worms, crayfish, and so on. Take the artificials and store them overnight with your live bait (night crawlers, wigglers, crayfish, and so forth). The artificials will pick up the natural scent of the live bait, making them more attractive to the fish.

INSTANT CHUM

One of the oldest methods of attracting fish is to use chum. Chum can be a variety of things, such as chopped-up baits, blood, and so forth, which are dumped into the water to entice fish to bite. It can also be some of the many food products found on your grocery shelves. The next time you're out fishing, try the following. Punch a few holes in a can of sardines or canned cat food and lower it over the side of the boat or through an ice-fishing hole. The oils and ingredients will spread out of the holes, attracting various species of fish.

FISHING STRATEGIES

The following are a few strategies to consider when you plan your next fishing trip.

SPRING FISHING
SELECTING A LAKE

When spring arrives, look to the smaller lakes in your area for the best results.

Most small lakes contain both shallow and deep-water struc- ture, and one or two bright days with mild temperatures can cause the shallow areas in these lakes to rise in temperature by five or ten degrees, triggering some great fishing.

USING CRANKBAITS

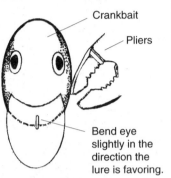

Crankbait

Pliers

Bend eye slightly in the direction the lure is favoring.

Before you go fishing, if you plan to use "crankbaits," try giving them a tune up. Cast your plug from the shore or a pier and as you retrieve, note which way it's running. If it comes back straight, it's ready to use. If it runs to the side, you need to bend the eye in the direction it's favoring. The adjustment should be very slight; otherwise you may over-com- pensate.

CANE POLIN' IN HEAVY WEED COVER

Cane pole fishing is an old fashioned technique and all-purpose method used to catch fish in heavy weed cover. In most cases, you use a 16-foot cane or fiberglass pole with a short line off the the tip to maintain control of the lure or bait that is worked in weedy pockets found in weedbeds, lily pads, or tough to reach areas.

You can use jigs, lures, spinners, or live baits, which can be dipped gently into a pocket and then worked with a swimming action or just plain jigged, using the conventional up and down technique.

Cane polin' may not be a glamorous way to fish, but it can't be beat for heavy weed cover.

SLOW FORWARD TROLLING

Try this technique on larger bodies of water such as the Great Lakes or any large reservoir. "Slow Forward Trolling" is used primarily during early spring-season fishing and on certain bodies of water during the summer and fall seasons.

Using a fairly stiff trolling rod with a 15 lb. test line (with a low stretch factor) and an 8 to 10 lb. test leader, rig the line as follows.

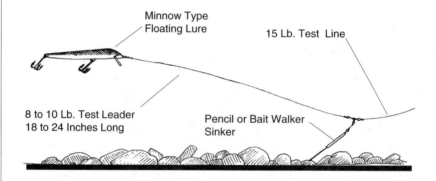

Minnow Type
Floating Lure

15 Lb. Test Line

8 to 10 Lb. Test Leader
18 to 24 Inches Long

Pencil or Bait Walker
Sinker

Attach any artificial floating minnow type lures such as Repalas, Rebels, and so forth, and position a sinker heavy enough to take the line and lure to the bottom approximately 18 to 24 inches ahead of the lure. The type of sinker to use will depend on the area to be trolled. For most situations, the more streamlined versions with the least water resistance should be used, and in rocky areas, Pencil types or Gapen's Bait Walkers work well.

Direction

Slow troll the rig so that the sinker occasionally makes contact with the bottom. The purpose of this is that it will establish the correct depth to fish and will also give you an indication of the bottom's composition. Once you hit a productive spot, keep the lure at the same depth on subsequent passes.

This method of trolling can be employed when it's too windy to back troll, or when you want to cover a large fishing area.

FISHING STRATEGIES

FISHING THE EDGES

Gamefish are "edge" oriented: they are attracted to places where an abrupt change occurs in their environment. Edges are underwater terrain where changes such as weed lines, gravel bars, bolders, logs, humps, or any submerged object changes the terrain. They can also be borders between rough and calm or discolored and clear waters. They can be shadows on the surface created by overhanging trees. They occur in many forms, and recognizing them takes skill.

Many types of fish-holding edges can be readily found by observent anglers, by simply looking around and taking note of the terrain and the water quality. Finding fish is 90% of successful fishing. Once you find them, catching them is easy.

HANG-UPS

If your presentation constantly gets snagged while you are fishing over a rocky bottom, add a slip bobber. Adjust the bobber so that your presentation hangs just above the rocks.

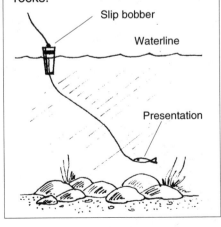

AQUATIC PLANTS

When working waters in early spring, keep an eye out for emerging cabbage plants. Cabbage plants in particular attract great numbers of bait fish, which in turn, attract predators. The newer the cabbage, the better the fishing. As the water temperature rises, cabbage plants sprout up within a few days and are easy to spot because of their light color. If you find some, don't pass them up.

HOOKING, PLAYING, AND LANDING TIPS

Regardless of the species, the proper techniques for hooking, playing, and landing your catch are essentially the same. The following are a few important reminders on how it's done.

SETTING THE HOOK

The first step necessary to catch a fish is to set the hook properly. Hooks must be set or driven into the fish's jaw. Rarely will a fish hook itself, or swallow the hook.

To set the hook, the angler should rear up and back with the rod fast and hard. This action should be repeated two or three times if it feels like a large fish.

PLAYING YOUR CATCH

After hooking a fish, a skilled angler plays a fish. He neither horses nor babies it; he applies pressure using his rod in a pump-and-reel technique to bring the fish to the net. To pump-and-reel, you drop the rod tip down to the water and reel in the line. Then you stop reeling, raise the tip, and repeat the lowering and reeling action. If the fish makes a run, give it line and repeat the pump-and-reel technique after it stops.

A common mistake made by many anglers while reeling is to reel in with the rod tip down near the water or with the rod in a horizontal position.

JUMPING FISH

To prevent losing your catch when it jumps, instantly lower your rod tip, giving slack line. When the fish falls back, it won't hit a taut line tearing out the hooks.

If it's headed for a snag, don't try to turn it by applying pressure or tightening the drag. Again, give it some slack. In most cases, if the fish no longer feels any resistance, it will stop running and turn away from the snag.

REELING IN YOUR CATCH

Never reel in your catch up to the rod tip. The proper way to reel in a hooked fish is to allow enough line to draw the fish across the water surface to your net or boat. You should stop reeling when you reach a line length that is a little less than your rod length. This will enable you to raise the rod tip up and back and guide the fish to the net.

LANDING TIPS

The following are just a few tips on how to remove hooks, measure your catch, and put fish on a stringer.

REMOVING HOOKS

When removing a hook from a fish you landed, try holding it belly up (upsidedown). It will struggle less, and there will be less chance of you getting hooked by the struggling fish.

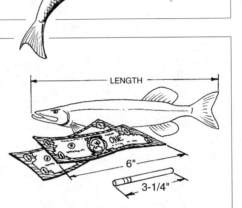

MEASURING YOUR CATCH

If you want to measure your catch and you don't have a ruler, just open your billfold and use any of the bills it contains. Ones, fives, tens, twenties, and so on are all six inches long and can be used as a ruler in a pinch.

If you are a smoker, you can also use a king-size cigarette, which is 3 1/4" long.

LENGTH

6"

3-1/4"

STRINGING TIPS

After you have made your catch, there's a proper way to string your fish to keep them alive and fresh as long as possible.

The following illustrations show the right way to string a fish with either a safety-pin-type or a bayonet-type stringer.

SAFETY-PIN-TYPE STRINGER

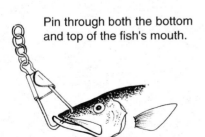

Pin through both the bottom and top of the fish's mouth.

BAYONET-TYPE STRINGER

WRONG WAY

Never string a fish through the gill as shown above.

RIGHT WAY

Pin through both the bottom and top of the fish's mouth.

AQUATIC PLANTS

Weeds are one of the most commonly found forms of structure in lakes, rivers, and streams. They provide cover for both predators and bait fish as well as other aquatic forms of life. Many game fish have a preference to specific types of weeds in their search for their next meal. The following information is a guide for identifying some of the more common submerged aquatic plants, which are good attractors of game fish.

CABBAGE

(Claspingleaf Pondweed)
The cabbage plant is both a deep or shallow water weed that has broad leaves and a brittle central stem. There are over 50 varieties of cabbage in North America. They vary in color from a light green to a reddish brown. Cabbage is also called pike weed, celery, redtop, or musky weed. Cabbage is preferred by both bass and pike over most other aquatic plants and it is the most productive aquatic plant for most game fish.

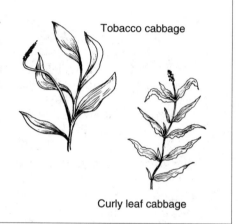

Tobacco cabbage

Curly leaf cabbage

COONTAIL

Coontail is a bushy-stemmed plant that grows in huge clumps or beds that form a canopy-type cover in shallow waters. It provides excellent cover for bait fish as well as other forms of aquatic creatures. Because of the bait fish, it also attracts most game fish species.

Coontail

WATER MILFOIL

Milfoil is similar to coontail as both have a bushy stem and are clinging plants. It grows in both shallow or deep water, and can be found mixed in with cabbage as well as coontail. It also attracts bait fish as well as game fish.

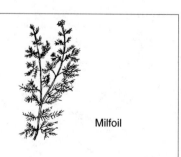

Milfoil

AQUATIC PLANTS

EEL GRASS

Eel grass is a long narrow-leafed plant that grows in shallow water. It is mostly found in flat sandy areas along the shoreline. Pike, pickerel, and bass favor eel grass during the summer season.

Eel Grass

CABOMBA

Cabomba is a long-stemmed plant similar to coontails or milfoil. It provides excellent cover for bait fish and other aquatic life. It forms tight beds over large areas, growing to within a foot of the surface. Because of its thick cover, cambomba attracts both panfish and predators.

Cabomba

SAND GRASS

Sand grass is a shallow water plant that grows on sandy flats to a maximum height of 18 inches. It is brownish green and brittle to the touch. Sand grass is also called musk grass or chara. Panfish are often found during their spawning season in the sandy flats containing sand grass.

Sand Grass

ELODEA

Elodea is another aquatic plant that is similar to milfoil. It attracts both bait fish as well as bass, and other predators. It has a long brittle stem with short leaves.

Elodea

AQUATIC PLANTS

LILY PADS
(Water Lily)

Lily pads consist of flat-leafed flowering plants that belong to the *(Nymphaeaceae)* water lily family. For the most part they are found growing along the shallower waters of the shoreline in sandy or soft-bottomed areas. In clearer lakes, they may grow to depths of 8 to 10 feet and can be very productive for largemouth bass. Lily pads and largemouth bass fishing are synonymous; however, all types of game fish can be found in the pads.

Lily Pads (Water Lily)

WATER HYACINTH

The water hyacinth is a floating short-rooted aquatic plant found in waterways in most southern states. It belongs in the lily family (Pontederiaceae) and grows in large tightly knit canopy-type clumps. It supports all types of aquatic life and is excellent for panfish or largemouth bass fishing.

Water Hyacinth

REEDS, BULRUSHES, AND CANE

Reeds, bulrushes, and cane are shallow-water plants with long broad leaves found growing along the shorelines of lakes, ponds, and streams. Reeds generally grow on firm bottoms, while bulrushes and cane are usually found on softer bottomed areas. Bass, pike, and musky are frequently found using these areas.

Reeds, Bulrushes or Cane

BUOY MARKERS

Buoy markers are used to mark hot spots when a fisherman plans to return to fish a location at a later time. They are left unattended with the expectation that the marker will still be there when the fisherman returns. However, many store-bought markers seem to disappear, which is basically the reason why many fishermen make their own. The following illustrations show a few examples of how to make your own simple marker buoys, which work as well as any store-bought markers.

HOW MARKERS WORK

Whether using a homemade marker such as the styrofoam cup or plastic bottle type (shown in the following illustrations) or one bought from a store, they all work the same. All they are is a float device with a cord and weight attachment.

When you want to mark a location, just drop it over the side and allow the weight to pull the line off until it reaches the bottom.

When you return, and you're all done, you simply pick it up and re-wind the line.

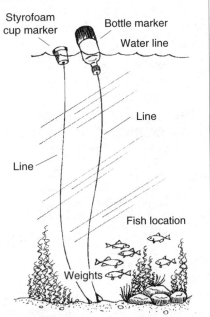

SMALL BOTTLE MARKER

STEP 1
Take two small 8 oz. fruit juice or soda pop containers and apply epoxy cement to both container mouths.

STEP 2
Secure containers with rubber bands while glue dries.

STEP 3
After glue dries, paint containers with bright fluorescent paint (optional). Next tie on a line, wind desired line length around container necks, and add sinker weight to the end of the line.

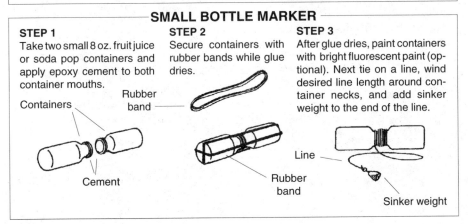

BUOY MARKERS

Here's a way to save yourself a few bucks by making your own marker buoys from empty two-liter plastic pop bottles or cheap styrofoam cups. All you need is some old fishing line, some weights (sinkers, rocks, or so forth), and a little time. Here's all you have to do.

PLASTIC BOTTLE MARKER

Step 1

Remove the cap from the bottle and using a heated nail or a drill, burn or drill a hole in the center of the bottle cap.

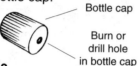

Bottle cap

Burn or drill hole in bottle cap

Step 2

Pass the line through the hole in the cap and tie a knot larger than the hole.

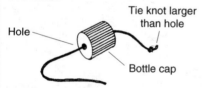

Tie knot larger than hole

Hole

Bottle cap

Step 3

Reattach the cap to the bottle and wind the remaining line around the bottle as shown in the diagram. Attach your weight (bank sinker, rock, or so forth) to the end of the line and your marker buoy is now complete.

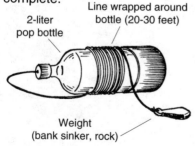

Line wrapped around bottle (20-30 feet)

2-liter pop bottle

Weight (bank sinker, rock)

STYROFOAM CUP MARKER

Step 1

Take a package of styrofoam cups and make a small hole in the bottom of each cup. Pull a string through the hole and tie the end to a match stick, nail, or so forth. Wind the line (desired length) around the cup and attach a weight (sinker, rock, washer, and so forth) to the end of the line.

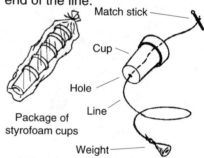

Match stick

Cup

Hole

Line

Package of styrofoam cups

Weight

Wind the line (desired length) around the cup and attach a weight (sinker, rock, washer, and so forth) to the end of the line.

Step 2

Using a marker pen, mark the line length on the lip of the cup as shown in the illustration. You can stack the cups one on top of the other, with the line lengths showing for quick reference.

Wound line

10 FEET

Line length

CHAPTER
2
BAIT

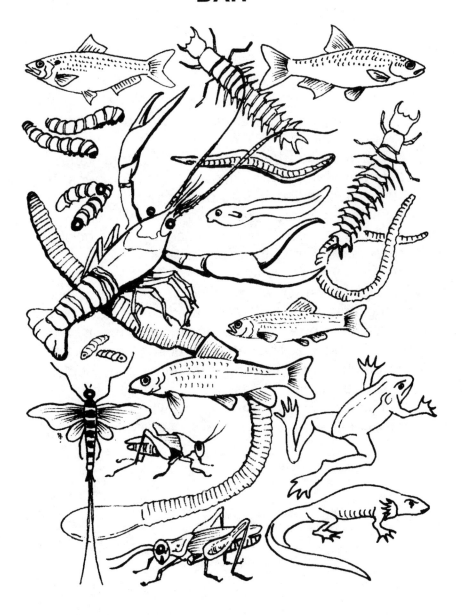

Bait Tips

The basic concern of all fish is cover and food for their existence.

The food can be almost anything from various aquatic or terrestrial animals to plants or other species of fish (including their own species).

Over the years, one of the more successful methods to catch fish was to use live baits or prepared baits. Both still remain as favorite methods to use today by many anglers.

Most fishermen at one time or another will use some form of live bait or prepared bait to catch fish.

In this chapter, I included the most common baits used for fishing. The pages cover some helpful tips on purchasing, collecting, preparing, and keeping the more common baits.

Also included are some tips on when and how to use them.

PURCHASING BAIT

The following are a few tips to remember when purchasing and using live baits.

- Always use fresh, spunky offerings when live bait fishing.
- If using leeches, change them frequently.
- When buying live bait, make certain it looks lively. Night crawlers and leeches should be firm; minnows and chubs should be swimming at the bottom of the tank rather than the top.
- Cool your bait bucket before you fill it.
- Don't over crowd your bait bucket.
- Don't put your bait in chlorinated water; use lake or well water.
- When fishing, keep your bait cool and out of the sun.

BAIT FISH

The following chart should be used when you purchase bait fish. One of the most important things to consider is how hardy and lively your bait fish will be and how long they will survive when you reach your fishing destination.

SPECIES	HARDINESS
Mud Minnows, Fathead Minnows, Madtoms	Most Hardy
Dances, Bluntnose Minnows, Creek Chubs, Suckers	Moderately Hardy
Golden Shiners, Roaches	Fairly Hardy
Alewifes, Ciscos, Shad, Smelt	Least Hardy

SIMPLE AERATOR

A few pieces of a dry red clay flowerpot dropped into your minnow bucket every so often will keep your bait alive and frisky on a long trip. Oxygen bubbles escaping from the clay chunks will aerate the water for several hours.

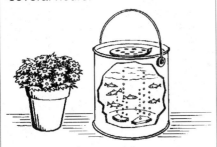

BUYING MINNOWS

A one-gallon bait bucket will hold one or two dozen small or medium size minnows. However, if you purchase larger bait fish like chubs, roaches, or suckers, a standard bait bucket will hold only four to eight fish.

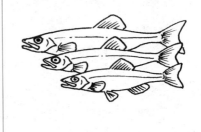

EARLY SPRING BAITS
March through April

Live baits are a super choice when you are fishing in early spring in the northern parts of the country. Most artificial baits require a fast or moderate retrieve to produce their proper action which, in most cases, will be too fast for the cold waters found in March through April.

Most northern cold-blooded fish are still in first gear and require a slow crawling retrieve to induce them to bite. The following are a few live bait choices to try for your favorite species during this time of the year.

Bluegills/Sunfish

Grubs, waxworms, maggots, Euro larvae, spikes, mousies

Perch/Crappies

2" long minnows

Walleye/Saugers

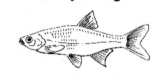

2" to 4" shiners, chubs

Largemouth/Smallmouth Bass

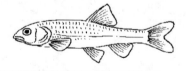

4" or better, shiners or chubs

Northerns/Muskie

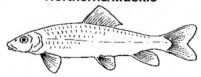

6" or better, suckers or chubs

BAIT FISH TIPS

Bait fish are one of the most extensively used live baits for fishing. The following are just a few tips relating to bait fish baits.

CASTING MINNOWS

Using a long shank #10 or #12 snelled hook, put the hook in the minnow's mouth and out one gill and then stick the point into its back at the base of the dorsal fin. The minnow will remain alive for quite some time when rigged in this manner. This technique can also be used with dead minnows, and in either case, dead or alive, after you cast, slowly reel in with a steady retrieve and an occasional jerk or twitch of the rod tip.

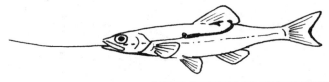

MIDAS TOUCH

If you want your ordinary shiners to have a golden hue like a golden shiner, place some dried red onion skins in the water along with the shiners and let them sit for a few hours or overnight. The water as well as the shiners will take on the color from the onion skins making the shiners more attractive to game fish.

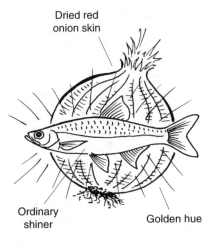

Dried red onion skin

Ordinary shiner

Golden hue

MINNOW SIZE

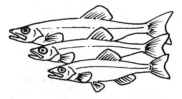

The following list is a general guideline for the best size minnow to use for a specific game fish.

Species	Minnow Size (inches)
Bluegill	1–2
Bullhead	3–6
Catfish	3–6
Crappie	1–2
Largemouth bass	3–6
Muskie	5–8
Northern pike	4–7
Perch	1–2
Pickerel	2–5
Rockbass	2–3
Smallmouth bass	3–5
Striped bass	3–6
Sunfish	1–2
Trout	1–4
Walleye	2–5

BAIT FISH TIPS

CATCH YOUR OWN

Have you ever run out of minnows during a fishing trip, or wished that you had brought some along? Well here's a tip for solving the problem. Next time you're out, take along or carry some tiny hooks (sizes #16 through #22) in your tackle box.

Just bait up one of these tiny hooks with a piece of sandwich bread or meat, or some of the aquatic life you can find on the underside of a lily pad, and fish the shallows. The baited hook will attract minnows and baby sunfish, which can be caught and used as bait for larger fish.

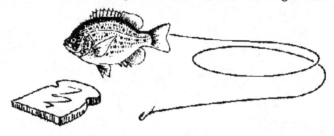

BAIT FISH TRAP

Here's a simple trap you can make to catch your own bait fish or other aquatic types of bait. All you need is an empty coffee can, some window screen material, and a stapler.

STEP 1

Cut a hole in the center of the plastic coffee can lid about 3 or 4 inches in diameter.

STEP 2

Form a tapered funnel using the window screen with a 1-inch diameter at the bottom and a large enough diameter at the top to fit around the hole in the plastic cover. The funnel should be about two-thirds the height of the can.

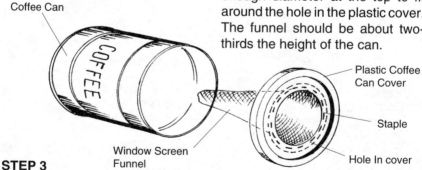

Coffee Can

Plastic Coffee Can Cover

Staple

Window Screen Funnel

Hole In cover

STEP 3

Staple the funnel to the plastic lid as shown in the illustration, and your trap is finished and ready to use. Bait the trap with pieces of bread and place it in the water around a weed bed or other type of cover where small bait fish congregate.

WORM TIPS

The following are just a few tips on collecting, keeping, and using worm baits.

COLLECTING WORMS

One of the eaisest ways to collect worms is to wait for a rain storm. After a heavy rain, worms will cover the sidewalks and driveways, just waiting to be picked up. To pick them up, try using a spatula; it is a lot easier and less messy. It is also best to wait 24 hours after the rain, because the worms will be less stressed out and tougher for fishing.

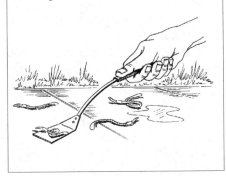

WHERE TO LOOK

Other places to look for worms are vacant lots, parks, and areas along river bottoms and the edges of creeks after the spring runoffs. These areas where the dry and the damp soils come together are excellent locations to find worms. Avoid golf courses or areas where commercial fertilizers have been used; worms cannot tolerate the chemicals in the fertilizer.

USING A FLASHLIGHT

When collecting at night, use a flashlight with a diffused beam (yellow or red cover) to spot worms. Bright lights drive them back into the ground.

CATCHING NIGHT CRAWLERS

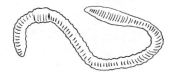

Here's a tip on how to grab a night crawler when you're out collecting for your next fishing trip. Don't grasp the head. Grab it near the rear part of the body where the worm comes out of the ground.

Once you've gotten hold of one, gently hold on without squeezing and slowly pull upward. Use a twisting motion and a steady pull to pop them out of their hole. Avoid excessive squeezing or pulling so as not to injure the worm. If you're careful when collecting, they will be more lively and last a lot longer.

FOOLING NIGHT CRAWLERS

In late spring, you can fool night crawlers into emerging from their holes if you pound a stake into the ground and rub another piece of wood across the stake top. The vibrations from rubbing the stake will bring the crawlers to the surface.

There are 1800 earthworm species throughout the world and they range in size from less than a half inch to as long as six feet. Of the 1800 species, 138 inhabit North America with many species being unique to a specific local. Simple as earthworms may seem, they are the most frequently used bait for fishing and probably the most productive.

WORM IDENTIFICATION

The following illustration shows the five most common worms used as bait.

Night Crawler
7 to 10 inches long
Color: Brownish pink to purplish red

Garden Worm
3 to 4 inches long
Color: Gray to yellow, sometimes bluish

Leaf Worm
3 to 4 inches long
Color: Brownish pink to purplish red

Manure Worm
3 to 4 inches long
Color: Red with whitish bands

Wiggler
2 inches long
Color: Red

WORM CARE

The following are a few tips on taking care of worms.

■ Don't overcrowd your worm container. Store the container in a cool place like an old refrigerator.

■ Worms eat their own weight in food each day. Make sure you feed them.

■ Only take the number of worms you plan to use during a day's fishing and keep the rest at home.

■ When transporting worms, cushion the container from vibrations to prevent injury during a long trip to your favorite fishing hole.

TOUGH WORMS

To toughen up your worms, fill a large bucket with drain holes and a fifty-fifty mixture of leaf mold and sawdust. Then add a couple of cups of washed wet sand and mix everything together. Place your worms in the bucket overnight, and they will be tough and ready to use the next morning.

HOMEMADE WORM THREADER

Here's a handy gadget you can make to thread either live or plastic worms onto a two-hook worm harness. All you need are the following items.

MATERIALS

- 2" piece of 1/4" diameter dowel rod
- 6" piece of aluminum or plastic tubing (smallest diameter you can find)
- Epoxy cement

ASSEMBLY

STEP 1

Starting with the dowel rod, drill a hole in the center large enough to insert the tubing.

Drill hole

STEP 2

Next, glue one end of a 6-inch long piece of tubing into the dowel rod.

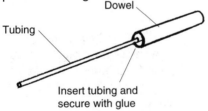

Dowel

Tubing

Insert tubing and secure with glue

STEP 3

After the tube is secured in the dowel rod, cut the opposite end of the tubing at an angle, giving it a sharp point.

Cut at angle

HOW IT WORKS

STEP 1

Stick the threader into the rear end of your night crawler and thread it through the middle of the worm and out the opposite end.

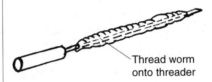

Thread worm onto threader

STEP 2

Hook the first harness hooks into the handle and insert the end hook into the hollow end of the tubing.

STEP 3

Work the worm back onto the harness up to the front hook and remove the hooks from the threader.

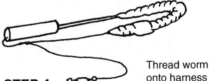

Thread worm onto harness

STEP 4

Work the front hook into the crawler, and arrange the back hook in the desired position.

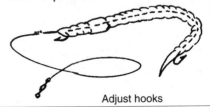

Adjust hooks

CRAYFISH TIPS

Crayfish have been one of the favorite baits used by live bait fishermen for catching perch, bass, and most any species of fish. They can be found in almost every type of lake, river, or stream throughout the United States, and for the most part they can be purchased in bait shops, The following are a few tips on using crayfish.

FISHING FOR SMALLMOUTHS

If you're going to be fishing for smallmouth bass, think crayfish. Studies have shown that crayfish are the favorite food of the smallmouth bass.

CATCHING CRAYFISH

The simplest way to catch crayfish is by turning over rocks in shallow water along the shoreline of a pond, lake, stream, or river and grabbing them by hand. However, after a few pinches, you may want to use a trap rather than your hands.

To make a trap, all you need is a wooden box attached to a string or rope, with a small opening at one end. The box should be weighted down with a few rocks and baited with beef or pork liver. It should be left overnight in a rocky or weedy area where crayfish congregate and checked the following morning.

KEEPING CRAYFISH

After you catch or purchase your crayfish, they should be kept in a styrofoam cooler, covered with wet grass or aquatic plants rather than a bait bucket. Crayfish in clusters of a dozen or more, require a lot of oxygen, and a cooler rather than a bucket will provide plenty. The cooler should be kept in a cool shady spot, and as long as the grass is wet and the crayfish don't dry out, they can be kept for days.

HOOKING CRAYFISH

The following illustration shows the best method to hook a crayfish to keep it lively and active when you are fishing.

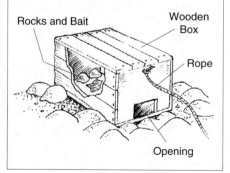

Rocks and Bait

Wooden Box

Rope

Opening

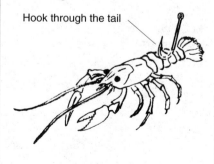

Hook through the tail

Leeches make excellent bait and have become very popular with walleye fishermen throughout the country. The following are a few tips on catching your own leeches, identifying them, and putting them onto hooks.

CATCHING LEECHES

In the spring, when the water in ponds, lakes, rivers, or streams reaches 50°, leeches become active and start searching for food. At this time they can be caught by using a simple trap which can be nothing more than an empty can baited with fresh beef liver or kidneys (with the top of the can crimped closed), or a baited gunnysack with a rope attached to it.

Place your trap in the weeds along the shoreline late in the day and pick it up prior to sunrise on the following day. Once you catch a few, they are easy to keep and will last a long time if you keep them in a bucket of water in a cool, dark place.

HOOKING

Fishing a leech is a relatively simple procedure. You can hook them on the back end of a jig or on a plain hook. However, to make them the most effective, you should hook them properly. Leeches are not to be hooked through the suction cup as most people think. It is best to hook the leech through the body right behind the suction cup.

Floating Jig or Lead Head Jig

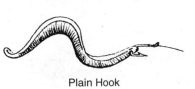

Plain Hook

LEECH IDENTIFICATION

Leeches are found in most waters throughout the northern United States, and the majority sold in bait shops come from Minnesota. Few fisherman know that some species of leeches are worthless as bait.

The two most commonly found leeches are the ribbon leech and the horse leech. Both are very similar in appearance making them difficult to identify. The best leech to use as bait is the ribbon leech, while the horse leech is worthless for fishing.

To determine which is which after you have collected leeches, simply fill a can halfway full of water, put in the leeches, and let it stand a while. The leeches that crawl out will be the horse leeches.

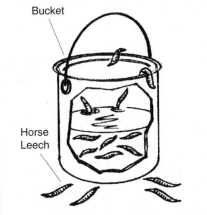

Bucket

Horse Leech

41

GRASSHOPPER/CRICKET TIPS

GRASSHOPPERS AND CRICKETS

Both grasshoppers and crickets are excellent baits for trout, bass, and most panfish. Here's a bait you can collect almost anywhere during the summer by just finding a grassy field. You can catch them by hand or with a net, and they are easy to keep. The following are a few tips regarding grasshoppers and crickets as bait.

CRICKET COLLECTING

Moisten and sprinkle a couple of pieces of bread with some sugar and cover them with a piece of cloth or newspaper. Leave it out over night, and the next day, lift the cloth or newspaper and collect the crickets

Moistened bread sprinkled with sugar

Newspaper

STORAGE

When you catch enough grasshoppers or crickets for a few outings, simply store them in a narrow-necked bottle with some grass or leaves. The narrow-necked bottle will make it easier to shake them out (one at a time) when you're out fishing. You can also keep them in a commercially manufactured bait box, which can be purchased at most bait or tackle shops.

RIGGING

They can be fished on the surface or below the surface using a fine wire hook, with the best place to hook them being through the collar just behind the head. When surface fishing, just cast to a likely spot and allow the bait to drift naturally. If you're fishing below the surface, clamp on just enough split shot twelve inches above the hook to sink your bait.

Narrow-necked pop bottle

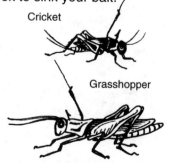

Cricket

Grasshopper

CATALPA WORMS

Most river fishermen know that if you turn a catalpa worm inside out, it is more effective. The following homemade tool is a handy gadget to have when using catalpa worms as bait. All you need to make the tool is a wire coat hanger and a pair of long nose pliers. Here's how you do it.

STEP 1
Cut out a 4- to 5-inch long wire from the coat hanger.
STEP 2
Form an eye on one end of the wire.
STEP 3
Tie a couple of feet of string to the eye and you're all finished.

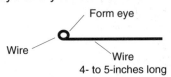

Form eye

Wire

Wire

4- to 5-inches long

HOW IT WORKS
To use the tool, tie the string to your waders or your belt so as not to lose it. Then take the tool and a worm and push the rod against the worms head, drawing the worm down the rod. Slip the worm off the rod, and put the worm onto the hook.

Wire

String   Catapla Worm

MAGGOTS (Spikes)

One of the best baits to use for panfish fishing is a maggot. It is an excellent bait for bluegill, sunfish, or rockbass. It can be used during any season and can be obtained in most bait shops throughout the country.

The maggot is the larvae of the blowfly and is considered the most sanitary bait sold in the United States. It carries no bacteria and is 100% protein. It can also be used for most any game fish including bass, stripers, walleye, trout, salmon, pike, and even musky. All fish, including the larger species, at some point in their lives eat insect larvae, which makes the maggot an excellent bait.

Keeping maggots alive is a simple process. When you are fishing, keep them out of the direct sunlight or in a cooler, and they will last the entire day. After you're done, put the remainder into a refrigerator to cool them down to a near motionless condition for use on another day. When maggots are cold and inactive, they retain their food supply longer, and will live longer.

They can be used for ice fishing, still fishing, jigging, and fly fishing. So the next time you're out, give them a try, and you may be surprised by the results.

PORK RIND TIPS

Pork rind baits are made from a hog's skin that is cut into various shapes, dyed various colors, and then preserved in a chemical solution. They can be used with almost any lure, spoon, jig, spinner bait, or by themselves, and are very effective for all game fish. The following are a few tips on using pork rind baits.

ATTACHMENT/REMOVAL

When using pork rind, most fishermen know how difficult it is to stick a hook through the tough skin. To solve the problem, most manufacturers have provided a simplified way to apply pork rind to the hook. The next time you use it, try drying the top colored side, and at the tip, you should find a small cut where you can easily hook it. You can also easily remove it by turning the hook sideways and pushing it off through the cut.

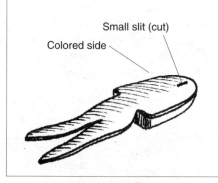

Colored side   Small slit (cut)

SEAM RIPPER

Another handy gadget to carry in your tackle box is a seam ripper used for sewing. This little item makes cutting a slit into the pork rind or removing it a lot easier.

EARLY SPRING PANFISH

A small spinner with a strip of pork rind trailing behind is an effective panfish lure during early spring. To improve its catching ability, attach a small bluegill hook to the trailing end of the pork rind as shown below.

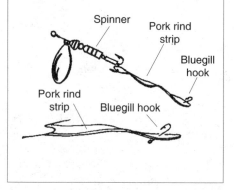

Spinner   Pork rind strip

Bluegill hook

Pork rind strip   Bluegill hook

LEAKY BOTTLES

To prevent your preserved bottled baits (such as pork rind, salmon eggs, and so forth) from leaking, simply slip a rubber band around the last thread of the jar and tighten down the lid.

UNCLE JOSH
PORK RIND BAIT

Rubber band

SOFT BAIT TIPS

The following are just a few tips for the fisherman who uses soft baits for catfish, carp, and so forth.

SOFT BAIT HOOK

Here's a simple way to make your plain hooks into some soft bait hooks that will improve their holding power.

Step 2
Cut the spring to the hook shank length and slip it onto the shank.

Step 1
Starting with a finishing nail, hold it with a pair of pliers or vise grips and wrap some soft wire around it to form a spring.

Step 3
When you bait up, just squeeze the bait on the spring and start fishing.

HOOKING SOFT BAITS

Here's a tip to keep your soft baits such as blood, cheese, or dough from slipping off the hook.

For the blood bait, soak a few cotton balls in the blood overnight. The soaked cotton balls will hold the blood scent longer and the congealed blood won't come off the hook as easily.

For your cheese and dough baits, mix in some cotton ball fibers, or some dried cattail fuzz (which you can substitute for the cotton) to help keep them on the hook.

DOUGH BAIT RECIPE

1/2 Cup Cornmeal
1/2 Cup Flour
1/4 Cup White Karo Syrup
3 Heaping Tablespoons Creamy Peanut Butter
2/3 Cup Water

COOKING INSTRUCTIONS

Using a small pot, mix and heat the water, syrup, and peanut butter mixture over a low flame. Next, mix the cornmeal and flour together while they are dry and then slowly add them into the liquid while constantly stirring. Cook the entire mixture (while you are stirring) until it becomes too thick to stir or all of the water is gone. After the dough cools, you can mix in some cotton ball fibers or cattail fuzz to help hold it on the hook.

PRESERVING SPAWN

SPAWN BAIT TIPS

Many types of fish roe (eggs) make excellent baits. When you catch a fish filled with eggs, you have an added bonus for future fishing trips if you preserve the roe and properly use it.

Most roe baits sold commercially are salmon, trout, or steelhead eggs; however, the roe from most any fish can be used as bait for other species of fish. The following are just a few tips on preserving roe and how to use it.

PRESERVING

 Starting with a freshly caught female fish, carefully open the stomach cavity and remove the ovarian membranes called skeins. Refrigerate them as soon as possible or pack them in ice until you're ready to start the preserving process. You can apply any of the following methods to preserve the eggs singularly or in clusters or sacks.

METHOD #1

Using fresh skeins or ones that were refrigerated, apply the following steps.

Step 1. Cut the skeins into usable chunks (clusters) and separate the chunks, allowing room between each cluster to dry.

Step 2. Refrigerate the clusters for eight to ten hours.

Step 3. Remove the clusters from the refrigerator and add the preservative, which consists of powdered borax. Place the clusters in a paper bag and add 2 to 3 cupfuls of the powder in the bag and shake it thoroughly.

Step 4. Remove the clusters from the bag and place them on a piece of newspaper and refrigerate them for another hour or two.

Step 5. When the clusters become firm, layer them in a tight fitted lid jar with powered borax between each layer. You can now keep them refrigerated for about two months, or you can freeze them for future use.

METHOD #2

The preservative used for this method is sodium sulfite, which can be purchased at any photo-supply store. This method eliminates the drying time in the refrigerator and adds a red color to the eggs.

Step 1. Place the clusters in a paper bag with the sodium sulfite as you did in method #1, shaking them until they are thoroughly covered. Sprinkle a layer of sodium sulfite on the bottom of the jar and add a layer of clusters.

Step 2. Again alternate a layer of clusters and a layer of sulfite filling the jar.

Step 3. After the jar is filled, screw the jar lid tight and refrigerate until you're ready to use.

METHOD #3

This method is the same as method #2 except that the preservative is different. The preservative consists of a mixture of equal parts of sugar, salt, and powdered borax. This method also produces a red color to the eggs.

SPAWN BAIT TIPS

METHOD #4

This method can be used for single eggs or clusters to make them firmer so they stay on the hook better.

Step 1. Mix a solution of brine by adding one part sugar (1 cup) to four parts salt in a gallon of water. Stir the solution until the salt and sugar dissolve, creating a super saturated solution.

Step 2. Place the eggs in the brine solution until they cure. You can tell when they are done by their texture, which will be firm and not shriveled or rubbery.

Step 3. Remove them from the brine, and store them in a jar in your refrigerator or freezer until your ready to use them.

METHOD #5

This is the simplest method of all.

Step 1. Spread the eggs one layer thick on a piece of wax paper allowing them to dry for a day or two until they become rock hard or all dried up.

Step 2. Place the dried eggs in an airtight container until you're ready to use them.

Step 3. A day before your next trip, tie up your spawn sacks as shown below using the dried eggs.

Step 4. Rinse the sacks well under water and refrigerate them over night. The next morning they will have reconstituted into semisoft clusters and will be ready to use.

RIGGING SPAWN BAITS

METHOD #1-Clusters

Mesh material

Egg cluster

Snip off access material

Wrap material around eggs and tie with thread.

Mesh material

METHOD #2-Single Eggs

Hook egg off center

Slide egg onto shank and turn (rotate) toward hook point.

Pull egg down onto hook point.

BAIT STORAGE TIPS

FREEZING BAITS

With the cost of live bait so high, here's a way to stretch your dollars. After a fishing trip, freeze your leftover minnows, chubs, hellgrammites, and crayfish. On later trips or Canadian trips where you can't bring in live bait, you can use your frozen baits, and they will still work great. The cost of any live bait up in Canada is out of sight, and in many places the selection is limited. By freezing your leftovers, you will have a ready-to-use variety of different baits.

FREEZING LEFTOVER BAIT

Freeze the baits in milk cartons (which you can also use in a cooler to cool your food), or in cling wrap packs of about one dozen per pack.

BAIT FREEZING TIP

If you're going to freeze your un-used baits in packets, roll the bait in cornmeal before you freeze it. When you go to use it, you can break off just what you need with-out thawing out the whole packet.

BAIT CONTAINER

Empty 35-mm plastic film con-tainers are great for holding small baits or lures such as pork rind strips, spikes, wax worms, small spinners, and so forth. They don't take up much room and easily fit into a pocket or tackle box. Be-sides that, if you drop one in the water, they float.

BAIT STORAGE TIPS

LIVE BAIT STORAGE CONTAINER

Here's a way to make a simple storage container that will allow you to keep a supply of minnows, chubs, or crayfish at home until you're ready to use them. All you need is a cheap styrofoam cooler (five-gallon capacity), an electric aerator, and a couple of pieces of wire screen.

ASSEMBLY

STEP 1

Starting with the cooler cover, decide on the location on the cover top for the aerator. Bore a hole in the cover, large enough to pass the aerator tube through.

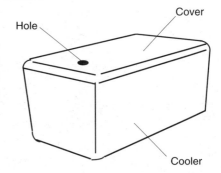

Hole
Cover
Cooler

STEP 2

Cut two pieces of screen (slightly oversize) to fit the inside width of the cooler as shown in the illustration at the right.

Note: The height of the screens should be short enough to compensate for the cooler cover when it's in place.

Compensate for cover
Screen (cut slightly oversize)
Cooler

SECTION VIEW
(Width of cooler)

STEP 3

Slip the screens into the desired locations, separating the cooler into three compartments.

Note: When the screens are inserted, the rough edges of the wire will dig into the styrofoam walls of the cooler, securing them in place.

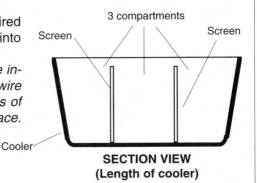

3 compartments
Screen
Screen
Cooler

SECTION VIEW
(Length of cooler)

ASSEMBLY (continued)

STEP 4

Place the container outside in a shady area out of the sun. Fill it with water and put in your minnows, chubs, and crayfish. Slip in the aerator tube through the cover hole to the bottom of the container and plug in the aerator.

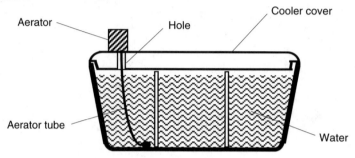

Aerator   Hole   Cooler cover

Aerator tube   Water

STEP 5

Every other day, check the water level and the condition of the bait. If necessary, freshen up the water by tipping the cooler and spilling some water out and adding new water with your garden hose.

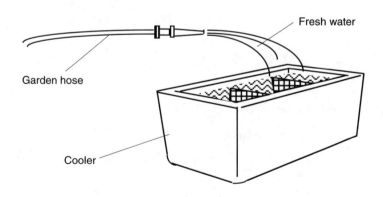

Fresh water

Garden hose

Cooler

CHAPTER
3

RIGGING

Rigging Tips

In this chapter, you will find some of the more successful ways to rig your equipment.

Whether you're bank fishing, still fishing, trolling from a boat, or using artificial baits, the following pages contain tips on rigging that can improve your ability to catch fish.

The rigs shown in this chapter have been used and tested by experienced anglers with exceptional results.

Many of the rig examples, shown on the following pages, are for specific fish species; however, in many cases they can be used for other species as well.

FISHING KNOTS

Every fisherman should take the time to learn how to tie the various knots listed in the chart below. Tying a good knot is one of the most important things required for a successful day's fishing. The following chart is a quick reference for selecting the more common knots to use when attaching hooks, flies, snaps, swivels, sinkers, lures, leaders, and various diameter lines to lines, or lines to reels.

Some helpful tips to remember when tying knots are as follows.
1. Use plenty of working line.
2. Tighten the knot with a steady, even motion.
3. Pull the knot tight.
4. Don't trim the tag end too close.

TYPE OF KNOT	ATTACHING							
	Hooks	Flys	Snaps or Swivels	Sinkers	Lures	Line to Line	Line to Leader	Line to Reel
World's Fair Knot	X	X	X	X	X			
Clinch Knot	X	X	X	X	X			
Polomar Knot	X	X	X	X	X			
Jansik Special	X	X	X	X	X			
Snell Knot	X							
Surgeon's Knot							X	
Blood Knot						X	X	
Albright Special						X	X	
Surgeon's End Loop	X	X	X	X	X	X	X	
Dropper Loop	X	X		X				
Perfection Loop	X	X	X	X	X	X	X	
King Sling	X		X		X			
Uni-Knot	X	X	X	X	X	X	X	X
Turle Knot	X	X	X	X	X			
Fisherman's Bend	X	X	X	X	X			
Fly Line Loop						X	X	
Two-Fold Open End	X	X	X	X	X			
Trilene Knot	X	X	X	X	X			
Shocker Knot						X		
Arbor Knot								X

RIGGING KNOTS-HOW TO TIE THEM

WORLD'S FAIR KNOT

Attaching: Hooks, snaps, swivels, lures, flies, and sinkers

Step 1. Form a six-inch loop and pass it through the eye.
Step 2. Bring the loop back and pull the doubled line through the loop.
Step 3. Pull the tag end under the double line.
Step 4. Bring the tag end back through the new loop.
Step 5. Pull the tag end and snug up the knot, sliding it to the eye, and clip the tag end.

Step 1

Step 2

Step 3

Step 4

Step 5

CLINCH KNOT

Attaching: Hooks, snaps, swivels, lures, flies, and sinkers

Step 1. Pass the line through the eye and make five turns around the line with the tag end. Then bring the tag end back and pass it through the big loop.
Step 2. Hold the tag end and snug up the coils with the standing line.

Step 1   **Step 2**

POLOMAR KNOT

Attaching: Hooks, snaps, swivels, lures, flies, and sinkers

Step 1. Form a loop and pass it through the eye.
Step 2. Tie a loose overhand knot with the double line.
Step 3. Pull the loop over the object (hook, swivel, lure and so forth).
Step 4. Tighten both the tag end and standing line.

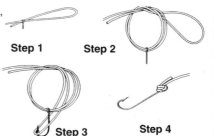

Step 1   **Step 2**

Step 3   **Step 4**

JANSIK SPECIAL

Attaching: Hooks, snaps, swivels, lures, flies, and sinkers

Step 1. Pass the line through the eye, forming a circle, and run it through the eye again.
Step 2. Make a second circle and pass the line through the eye a third time.
Step 3. Bring the tag end around in a third circle and wrap it three times around the other two circles and the third circle with three wraps.
Step 4. Tighten both the tag end and standing line by holding the object with one hand, the tag end with your teeth, and the standing line with your other hand.

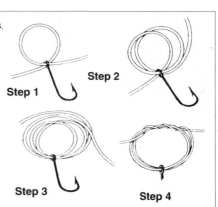

Step 1   **Step 2**

Step 3   **Step 4**

54

RIGGING KNOTS-HOW TO TIE THEM

SNELL KNOT

Attaching: Hooks

Step 1. Pass the line through the eye, forming a loop, and run it through the eye again in the opposite direction.

Step 2. Take the part of the loop closest to the eye and wrap it over the shank and tag end giving it seven or eight turns.

Step 3. Holding the working line with your right hand, and the wraps with your left, slowly and steadily pull the standing line until the knot is almost tight. Then grasp the tag end with your fingers or a pair of pliers and pull it and the standing line at the same time until the knot is tight.

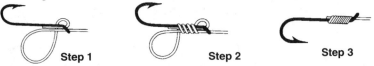

Step 1   Step 2   Step 3

SURGEON'S KNOT

Attaching: Leaders to line

Step 1. Lay the leader and line parallel to each other with the ends overlapping by six or eight inches. Then tie an overhand knot passing the entire leader through the loop.

Step 2. Leaving the overhand knot loop open, pull the tag ends of both lines through the loop.

Step 3. Holding both lines and the tag ends, pull the knot tight.

Step 1   Step 2   Step 3

BLOOD KNOT

Attaching: Leader to leader or leader to line

Step 1. Lay the two lines parallel to each other with the ends overlapping by six or eight inches. Then grip the two lines at the midpoint with one hand and begin wrapping the tag end of one of the lines around the other line (at least five turns), bringing the tag end to the mid-point and passing it between both lines.

Step 2. Changing hands, repeat the procedure with the other tag end while holding the lines at the midpoint.

Step 3. Bring the tag end of the second line and insert it between the lines at the midpoint in the opposite direction of the other line.

Step 4. Letting go of the tag end, pull both standing lines in the opposite directions to tighten the knot.

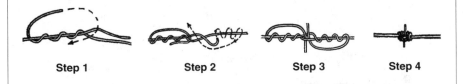

Step 1   Step 2   Step 3   Step 4

ALBRIGHT SPECIAL

Attaching: Line to line, line to leader

Step 1. Form a loop with the tag end of the heavier line, holding it with your thumb and forefinger. Pass the other line through the loop.

Step 2. Pinch the tag end of the lighter line with your thumb and finger against the heavier line and wrap it around both lines over itself.

Step 3. Take at least twelve wraps around the loop with the lighter line going forward toward the end of the loop and slip the tag end through the loop.

Step 4. With your thumb and forefinger, slide the coils toward the end of the loop.

| Step 1 | Step 2 | Step 3 | Step 4 |

SURGEON'S END LOOP

Attaching: Hooks, snaps, swivels, lures, flies, line to line, leader to line and sinkers

Step 1. Double the end of the line and form a loop, then tie a loose overhand knot at the end of the doubled line.

Step 2. Bring the doubled line (loop) around and through the overhand knot.

Step 3. While holding the standing line and the tag end, pull the loop to tighten the knot.

| Step 1 | Step 2 | Step 3 |

DROPPER LOOP

Attaching: Hooks, flies, and sinkers

Step 1. Form a loop in the line, then with the tag end, give it about eight to ten turns around the standing line.

Step 2. Find the center of the turns, and pull the remaining loop through.

Step 3. Hold the loop using your teeth, and pull both ends of the line tightening the coils.

| Step 1 | Step 2 | Step 3 |

PERFECTION LOOP

Attaching: Hooks, snaps, swivels, lures, flies, line to line, leader to line and sinkers

Step 1. Take one turn around the line, forming a loop.

Step 2. Take a second turn around the cross point and bring the end around once more between the turns forming a second loop.

Step 3. Pass the second loop through the first loop.

Step 4. Holding the second loop, pull slowly until the knot jams.

Step 5. Finish the knot by trimming the tag end.

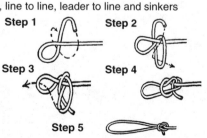

Step 1 Step 2 Step 3 Step 4 Step 5

RIGGING KNOTS-HOW TO TIE THEM

KING SLING

Attaching: Hooks, snaps, swivels, lures

Step 1. Insert the line through the eye (lure or so forth) and double back about ten inches.
Step 2. Form a loop with the double line and twist it four times around the double line.
Step 3. Bring the eye (lure or so forth) through the loop.
Step 4. Tighten the knot by pulling from both ends.

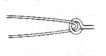

Step 1   **Step 2**   **Step 3**   **Step 4**

UNI-KNOT

Attaching: Hooks, snaps, swivels, lures, flies, line to line, leader to line, sinkers

Step 1. Insert the line through the eye (lure or so forth) and double back about six inches, bringing the end back in a circle.
Step 2. Make six turns around the double line and insert the end into the circle.
Step 3. Hold the double line at the eye and pull the tag end to snug up the turns.
Step 4. Slide the knot up against the eye and trim the tag end.

Step 1   **Step 2**   **Step 3**   **Step 4**

TURLE KNOT

Attaching: Hooks, snaps, swivels, lures, flies, sinkers

Step 1. Insert the line through the eye and tie a single running knot at the end of the line, forming a loop.
Step 2. Pass the fly or hook through the loop.
Step 3. Pull the knot tight behind the eye.
Step 4. Snip off the tag end.

Step 1   **Step 2**

Step 3   **Step 4**

FISHERMAN'S BEND

Attaching: Hooks, snaps, swivels, lures, flies, sinkers
Step 1. Pass the line through the eye twice and slip the tag end through both loops. Tie an overhand knot at the tag end and snug up the knot and trim the tag.

FLY LINE LOOP

Attaching: Leaders to fly lines
Step 1. Slip the leader loop over the fly line loop, and pull the end of the leader through the fly line loop.

TWO-FOLD OPEN END

Attaching: Hooks, snaps, swivels, lures, flies, sinkers

Step 1. Double the line at the tag end forming a loop. Tie a loose overhand knot with the loop forming a circle. Pass the loop around the double lines of the circle a second time.

Step 2. Snug up the knot with a steady pull while holding the loop and pulling the standing line. Trim the tag end.

Step 1

Step 2

TRILENE KNOT

Attaching: Hooks, snaps, swivels, lures, flies, sinkers

Step 1. Run the line twice through the eye.
Step 2. Loop the line around the standing line five or six times.
Step 3. Thread the tag end back through the coils at the eye.
Step 4. Pull the knot tight and trim the tag end.

Step 1   **Step 2**   **Step 3**   **Step 4**

SHOCKER KNOT

Attaching: Heavier lines to lighter lines

Step 1. Make an overhand knot at the end of the light line, and pull it tight. Next make a loose overhand knot at the end of the heavy line and pass the light line through the loose overhand knot.
Step 2. Tighten the overhand knot in the heavy line, and trim off the tag.
Step 3. Make three wraps around the heavy line with the light line and pass the end back through the first loop. Pull the light line tight, and trim off the tag.

Step 1   **Step 2**   **Step 3**

ARBOR KNOT

Attaching: Lines to reels

Step 1. Pass the line around the reel arbor.
Step 2. Tie an overhand knot around the standing line.
Step 3. Tie a second overhand knot at the tag end.
Step 4. Pull tight and snip off the excess at the tag end and snug down the first knot on the arbor.

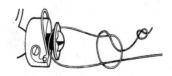

GREAT LAKES SALMON/ TROUT RIGS

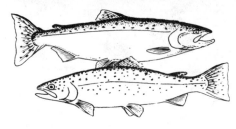

The following bait rigs are for fall trout or salmon fishing at the warm water discharges found at many of the power plants throughout the Great Lakes. They can be fished from shore or from a boat using smelt, minnows, or alewives as the bait.

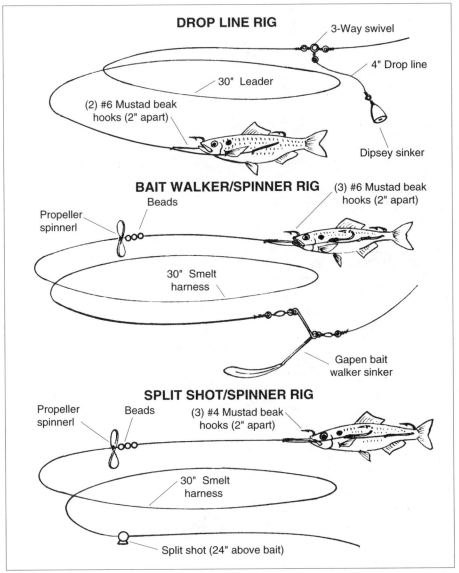

DROP LINE RIG

3-Way swivel

4" Drop line

30" Leader

(2) #6 Mustad beak hooks (2" apart)

Dipsey sinker

BAIT WALKER/SPINNER RIG

(3) #6 Mustad beak hooks (2" apart)

Beads

Propeller spinnerl

30" Smelt harness

Gapen bait walker sinker

SPLIT SHOT/SPINNER RIG

Propeller spinnerl

Beads

(3) #4 Mustad beak hooks (2" apart)

30" Smelt harness

Split shot (24" above bait)

WALLEYE RIGS

The next time you're out walleye fishing, try some of the following rigs.

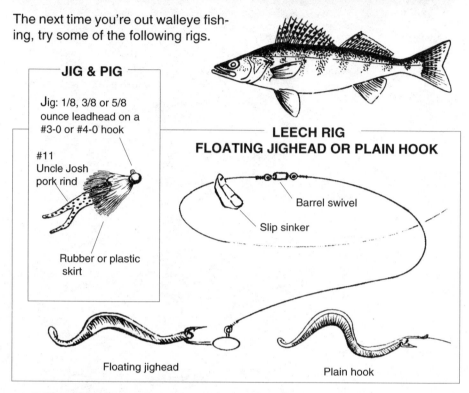

JIG & PIG

Jig: 1/8, 3/8 or 5/8 ounce leadhead on a #3-0 or #4-0 hook

#11 Uncle Josh pork rind

Rubber or plastic skirt

LEECH RIG
FLOATING JIGHEAD OR PLAIN HOOK

Barrel swivel

Slip sinker

Floating jighead

Plain hook

BOTTOM BOUNCING RIGS

The following rigs are very effective for walleye fishing when you are bottom bouncing in rocky areas. They can be baited with minnows, leeches, or worms.

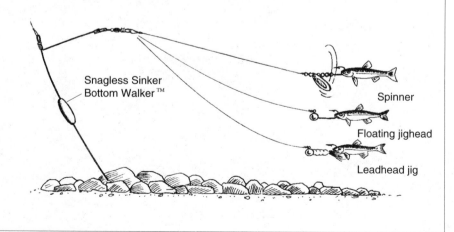

Snagless Sinker
Bottom Walker™

Spinner

Floating jighead

Leadhead jig

The following rigs are for walleye fishing when the walleye are suspended at various distances off the bottom. Each of the rigs can be adjusted to a specific depth.

ADJUSTABLE LEADER RIG

Rig Content: Floating jlg, adjustable float, bobber stop and bead, "Lindy" slip sinker and live bait.

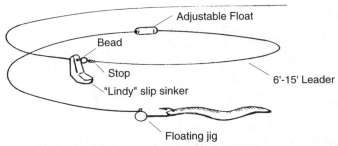

Adjustable Float

Bead

Stop

"Lindy" slip sinker

6'-15' Leader

Floating jig

ADJUSTABLE DROPLINE RIG

Rig Content: #6 short shank hook, bead and bobber stop, barrel swivel, drop line, bullet sinker, split shot, and live bait.

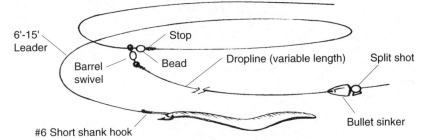

6'-15' Leader

Stop

Barrel swivel

Bead

Dropline (variable length)

Split shot

Bullet sinker

#6 Short shank hook

FIXED LEADER RIG

Rig Content: #6 short shank hook, adjustable float, barrel swivel, "Lindy" slip sinker, and live bait.

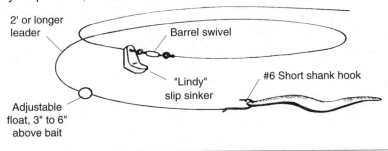

2' or longer leader

Barrel swivel

"Lindy" slip sinker

#6 Short shank hook

Adjustable float, 3" to 6" above bait

PIKE/MUSKIE FISHING

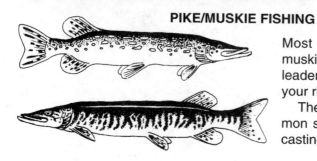

Most fishermen who fish for muskie or pike know that a wire leader is a must when you set up your rig.

The following rigs are common setups used for both lure casting or live bait fishing.

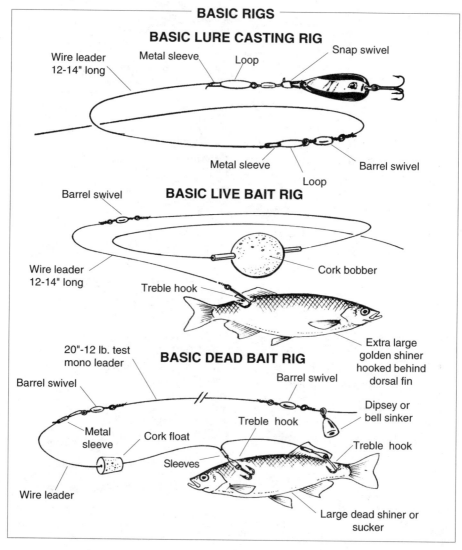

BASIC RIGS

BASIC LURE CASTING RIG

Wire leader 12-14" long
Metal sleeve
Loop
Snap swivel

Metal sleeve
Loop
Barrel swivel

BASIC LIVE BAIT RIG

Barrel swivel

Wire leader 12-14" long

Cork bobber

Treble hook

Extra large golden shiner hooked behind dorsal fin

BASIC DEAD BAIT RIG

20"-12 lb. test mono leader

Barrel swivel

Barrel swivel

Dipsey or bell sinker

Treble hook

Metal sleeve
Cork float

Treble hook

Sleeves

Wire leader

Large dead shiner or sucker

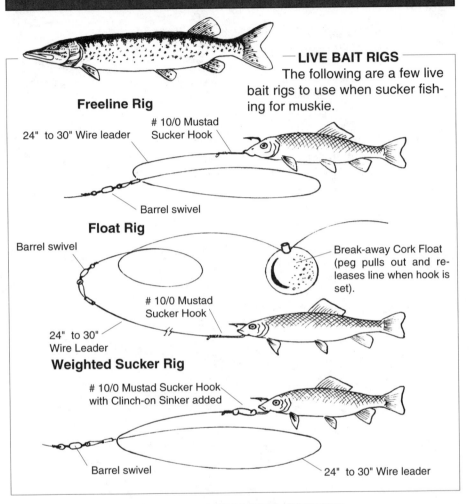

LIVE BAIT RIGS

The following are a few live bait rigs to use when sucker fishing for muskie.

Freeline Rig

10/0 Mustad Sucker Hook

24" to 30" Wire leader

Barrel swivel

Float Rig

Barrel swivel

Break-away Cork Float (peg pulls out and releases line when hook is set).

10/0 Mustad Sucker Hook

24" to 30" Wire Leader

Weighted Sucker Rig

10/0 Mustad Sucker Hook with Clinch-on Sinker added

Barrel swivel

24" to 30" Wire leader

SUCKER RIGGING FOR CASTING

Here's a way to rig a sucker for casting that will keep it on the hook. Starting with a short piece of line, pass one end of the line through the sucker's mouth and out through the side of the gill. Then bring the line over to the opposite side and thread it through the opposite gill and out the mouth. Hook the sucker through the mouth, and then snug up the thread from the mouth and tie it to the hook as shown below.

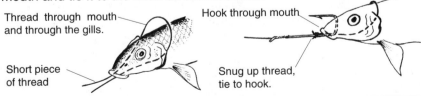

Thread through mouth and through the gills.

Hook through mouth

Short piece of thread

Snug up thread, tie to hook.

63

STRIPER RIGS

STRIPER FISHING

With the introduction of the saltwater striped bass to various reservoirs, lakes, and impondments throughout the country, striper fishing has become a bass fisherman's dream come true.

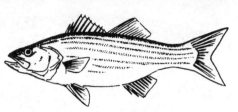

Fish over 50 pounds have been caught in many of the reservoirs or lakes containing these monsters. One of the best methods to catch stripers is by deep-water trolling. The following are a few examples of deep-water trolling rigs to try when fishing for stripers.

STRIPER TROLLING RIGS

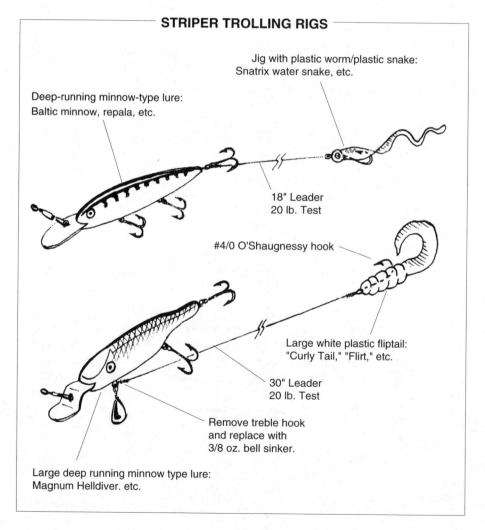

Jig with plastic worm/plastic snake: Snatrix water snake, etc.

Deep-running minnow-type lure: Baltic minnow, repala, etc.

18" Leader 20 lb. Test

#4/0 O'Shaugnessy hook

Large white plastic fliptail: "Curly Tail," "Flirt," etc.

30" Leader 20 lb. Test

Remove treble hook and replace with 3/8 oz. bell sinker.

Large deep running minnow type lure: Magnum Helldiver. etc.

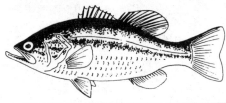

The following are the two most popular bass rigs used today. Both rigs are very productive when used properly. The following illustrations show how to set up your rig, and when and how to set the hook after you get a strike.

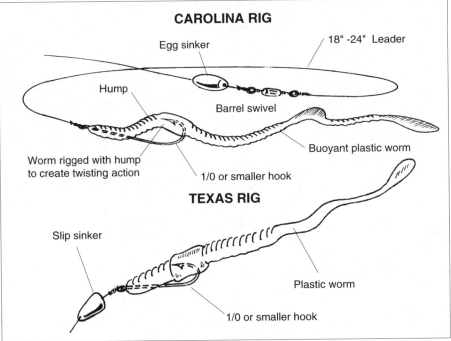

CAROLINA RIG

Egg sinker

18" -24" Leader

Hump

Barrel swivel

Worm rigged with hump to create twisting action

Buoyant plastic worm

1/0 or smaller hook

TEXAS RIG

Slip sinker

Plastic worm

1/0 or smaller hook

WHEN TO SET THE HOOK USING PLASTIC WORMS

To be a good plastic worm fisherman, you need to get out fishing as often as possible using plastic worm baits and experience worming.

With a lot of practice, you begin to feel and know when to jerk the line to set the hook. When fishing with plastic worms, most strikes will occur when the worm falls back or when it hits the bottom during the retrieve. Rarely will you get a strike after you have picked up the slack during the retrieve.

The strike will be a slight tap or peck, at which time the hook should be set.

To set the hook, lower the rod tip and snap the rod back with the wrist and forearm coming straight up rather than back until you almost hit yourself right in the face.

Plastic worm fishing requires the fisherman to watch his or her line, so he or she can feel and see the tap or peck when the fish strikes.

Again, only with a lot of practice, will you know when to set the hook.

LARGEMOUTH BASS RIGS

Anyone who fishes for bass knows how effective the plastic worm is. It's the most versatile lure on the market today, and it can be used in virtually any cover or any depth. The following are a few examples of ways to rig your plastic worms and how to use them.

PLASTIC WORM RIGS

A. Slider Rig: Midwater/ Drop-offs, rocky shorelines/Swimming action

B. Flipping Rig: Top water/Piers, docks, lily pads/Swimming action

C. Texas Rig: Any depth/Any condition/Bottom bouncing action

D. Swimming Rig: Top water/Heavy cover, lily pads/Swimming action

E. Skipping Rig: Top water/Heavy cover/Swimming action

F. Split Shot Rig: Midwater or just below the surface/Swimming Action

G. Jig Head Rig: Deep water/Drop-offs, rocky bottoms/Bouncing Action

H. Eufaulla Rig: Bottom Fishing/Mud flats, gravel bottoms/Short drags

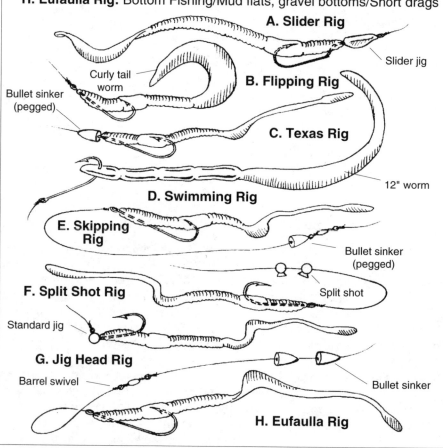

A. Slider Rig
Slider jig
Curly tail worm
Bullet sinker (pegged)
B. Flipping Rig
C. Texas Rig
12" worm
D. Swimming Rig
E. Skipping Rig
Bullet sinker (pegged)
F. Split Shot Rig
Split shot
Standard jig
G. Jig Head Rig
Barrel swivel
Bullet sinker
H. Eufaulla Rig

CURLY TAIL RIG

The following rig is an excellent setup for most panfish. It works well with bluegills, crappies, white/yellow bass, or most any other panfish. It can be worked with either a fast or slow retrieve, using small jigs or small hooks dressed with curly tails and rigged as shown below.

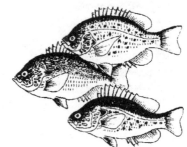

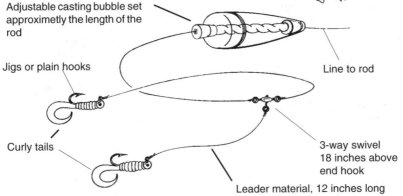

Adjustable casting bubble set approximetly the length of the rod

Jigs or plain hooks

Line to rod

Curly tails

3-way swivel
18 inches above
end hook

Leader material, 12 inches long

SLIP BOBBER RIG

The slip bobber rig is the most frequently used rig for most panfish. It can be fished in both deep and shallow water by simply adjusting the stop above the bobber. It can be rigged with jigs or plain hooks and baited with a variety of offering such as minnows, worms, crustaceans, and insects. The following illustration shows the proper way to rig a slip bobber.

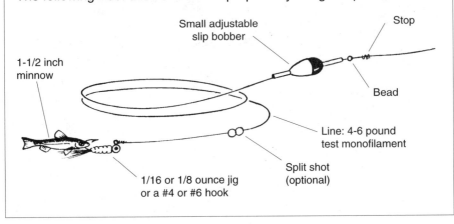

Small adjustable
slip bobber

Stop

1-1/2 inch
minnow

Bead

Line: 4-6 pound
test monofilament

1/16 or 1/8 ounce jig
or a #4 or #6 hook

Split shot
(optional)

BASS/PANFISH RIG

Here's a rig that packs a double whammie. All bass fishermen know that bass normally strike the front of a worm, and bluegills and most panfish strike the tail.

With the following setup, you can get a shot at both of them with the same rig.

Tie on your worm hook about 6 inches above the end of the line. Next tie on a small panfish hook at the end of the line.

Attach your worm onto the worm hook, and hook the small panfish hook into the tail end of the worm. Now you're ready for both bass and panfish.

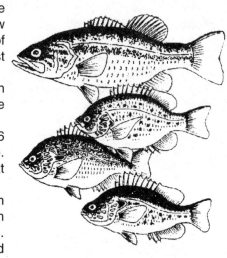

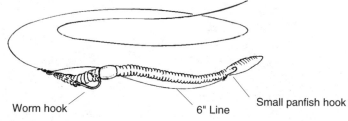

Worm hook   6" Line   Small panfish hook

CARP AND CATFISH RIG

Here's an effective rig for both carp and catfish. Tie on a floating jighead and pinch on a small clinch-on sinker about six inches above the jighead. The sinker should be just heavy enough to keep the jighead off the bottom.

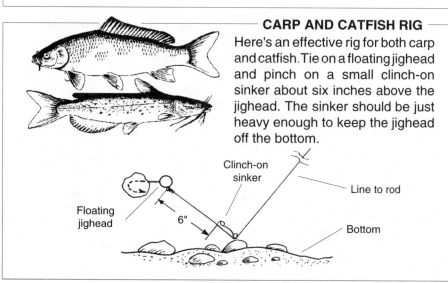

Clinch-on sinker

Line to rod

Floating jighead

6"

Bottom

Whether fishing from the shore or from a boat, the following rigs can be used for either catfish or bullheads. When baited with worms, stinkbaits, blood baits or baitfish, all of the rigs shown have proven to be very effective. Both catfish and bullheads are attracted to the bait by their sense of smell; therefore, the smellier the bait you use, the better the results.

The slip bobber rig can be set at various depths simply by adjusting the stop, while the other rigs can be used to drift or bottom fish. Both species are good fighters on light tackle and are excellent table fare.

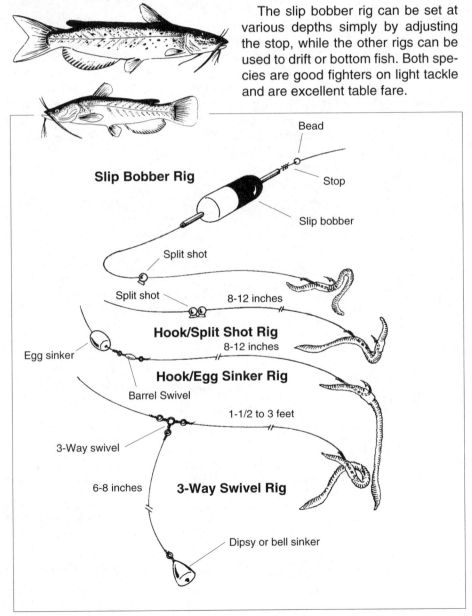

Slip Bobber Rig

Bead

Stop

Slip bobber

Split shot

Split shot

8-12 inches

Hook/Split Shot Rig

8-12 inches

Egg sinker

Hook/Egg Sinker Rig

Barrel Swivel

1-1/2 to 3 feet

3-Way swivel

6-8 inches

3-Way Swivel Rig

Dipsy or bell sinker

CRAPPIE FISHING

One of the key factors for successful crappie fishing is to use a light line (2 to 6 lbs. test) and small hooks (#6-#8) or jigs (1/3 to 1/8 ounce).

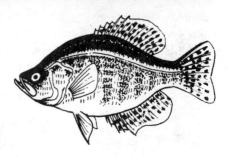

When using plain hooks, dress them with live baits such as minnows, grubs, or wax worms. With jigs, try different colors such as chartreuse, white, yellow, and purple. If you're not having any luck with one color, switch to another until you find the right one. You can dress the jigs with twister tails, fur, feathers (such as marabou), or you can also add live baits (minnows, grubs, and so forth). You can cast the jigs and bounce them along the bottom, swim them, or just plain jig them in both deep or shallow water.

Crappies, for the most part, will strike a moving bait, and when they do strike, the offering will be above them. The following are a few examples of how to rig your equipment for crappie fishing.

BASIC RIGGINGS

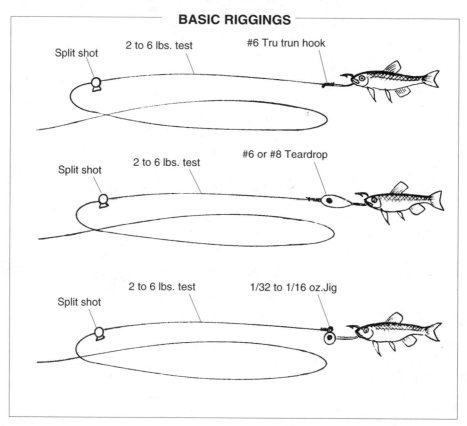

SPRING CRAPPIES

During the spring months (March/April) crappies are the most active and provide excellent fishing. The following are a few rigs to try using small hooks or jigs and small minnows.

DEEP WATER RIG

The rig consists of using 2 to 4 pounds test line with a 1/2 ounce bell or dipsey sinker tied to the end with two dropper lines 12 feet apart using lightweight hooks such as #6 or #8 gold Aberdeens, tied in 12 to 24 inches above the sinker (see diagram). The distance between the hooks should stay constant (12 inches); however, the distance from the sinker to the hook can vary from 18 to 24 inches if you're fishing in heavy brush.

SHALLOW WATER RIG

This rig consists of simply adding a float, or bobber, at the desired depth you want the jig to be (depth can be varied). You can use a plain jig, or you can dress it with a small minnow. The rig is then cast around weed beds and brush piles, using a slow retrieve, and twitching the rod tip as you reel in.

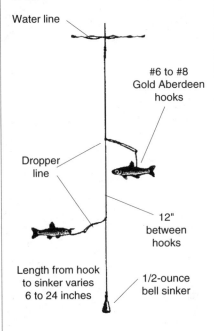

Water line

#6 to #8 Gold Aberdeen hooks

Dropper line

12" between hooks

Length from hook to sinker varies 6 to 24 inches

1/2-ounce bell sinker

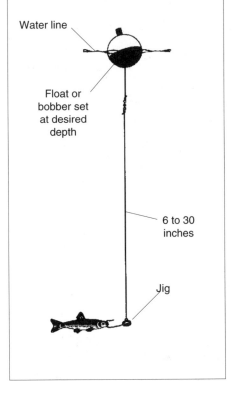

Water line

Float or bobber set at desired depth

6 to 30 inches

Jig

BOBBER FISHING

One of the more frequently used methods of fishing is using a bobber. Most of us as smallfry were introduced to fishing using bobbers because they were an easy way to rig and dangle a bait under a fish's nose.

Even today, fathers introduce their children to fishing using the bobber method. However, many American fishermen frown on using bobbers because they think bobbers are only for kids or rank amateurs.

On the other hand, many knowledgeable European anglers carry an array of bobbers and use them successfully. Today, bobber fishing is a sophisticated and effective fishing tool when it's used properly at the right time and place. Bobbers come in many different sizes and shapes and are attached to the line in a variety of ways. The following are only a few illustrated methods of rigging select bobber types that have proven to be very effective.

BOBBER RIGS

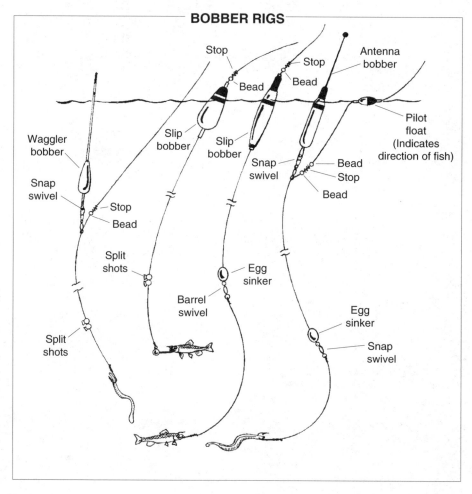

BANK FISHING RIG

Here's a way to keep your reels and rods clean rather than having them clogged up with sand, grit, or crud when bank fishing.

BANK FISHING SETUP

Step 1. The next time you buy something that comes with styrofoam packing, don't throw the styrofoam away. Before your next trip, make yourself a handful of " styrofoam bite indicators" by using a razor blade and cutting the styrofoam into small one-inch squares. Then cut a slit into each piece for your line as shown in the illustration below.

Step 2. After you arrive at your fishing location, find a bush or tree and cut off a couple of branches and make two Y-shaped sticks.

Step 3. Select the location along the bank where you plan to fish and push the Y-shaped sticks into the ground with one behind the other as rests for your rod handle and the rod.

Step 4. Cast out your baited line and place the rod in the Y of each stick as shown in the illustration. *Note: After you make your cast, leave the reel bail open.*

Step 5. Take the slack out of the line and place a small pebble on the line to keep the line taut.

Step 6. Attach the styrofoam indicator to the line at the tip of the rod.

When fishing, keep an eye on the indicator; when it moves, set the hook.

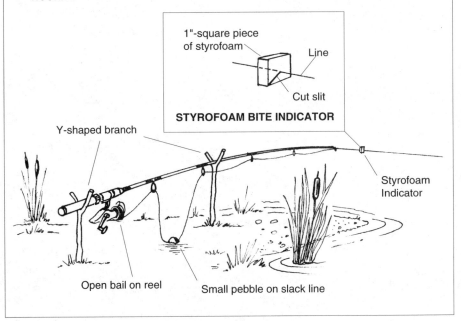

1"-square piece of styrofoam

Line

Cut slit

STYROFOAM BITE INDICATOR

Y-shaped branch

Styrofoam Indicator

Open bail on reel

Small pebble on slack line

TROLLING RIGS

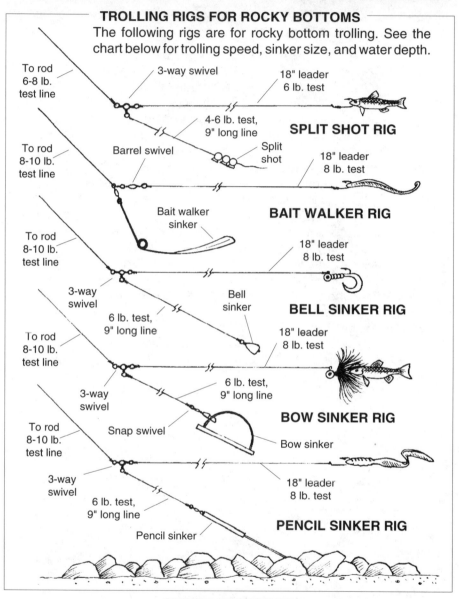

TROLLING RIGS FOR ROCKY BOTTOMS

The following rigs are for rocky bottom trolling. See the chart below for trolling speed, sinker size, and water depth.

To rod 6-8 lb. test line

3-way swivel

18" leader 6 lb. test

4-6 lb. test, 9" long line

SPLIT SHOT RIG

To rod 8-10 lb. test line

Barrel swivel

Split shot

18" leader 8 lb. test

BAIT WALKER RIG

Bait walker sinker

To rod 8-10 lb. test line

3-way swivel

18" leader 8 lb. test

6 lb. test, 9" long line

Bell sinker

BELL SINKER RIG

To rod 8-10 lb. test line

3-way swivel

18" leader 8 lb. test

6 lb. test, 9" long line

BOW SINKER RIG

Snap swivel

Bow sinker

To rod 8-10 lb. test line

3-way swivel

18" leader 8 lb. test

6 lb. test, 9" long line

Pencil sinker

PENCIL SINKER RIG

SINKER SELECTION

Trolling Speed	Trolling Depth			
	15' & Under	15'-25'	25'-40'	40' or Deeper
Slow	1/8-1/4 oz.	1/4-3/8 oz.	3/8-1/2 oz.	3/4 oz.
Moderate	1/4 oz.	3/8 oz.	1/2 oz.	1/2-3/4 oz.
Fast	3/8 oz.	1/2 oz.	1/2-3/4 oz.	-------------

CHAPTER
4

PRESENTATION

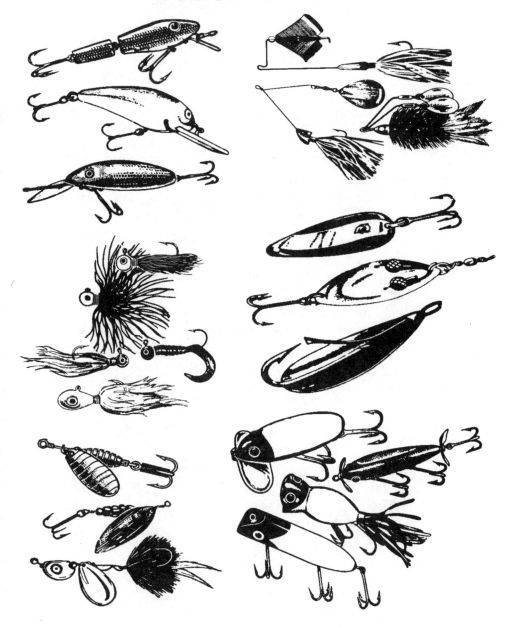

Presentation Tips

Spinning, bait casting, fly fishing, or just plain bait fishing all require a good presentation to catch fish. Regardless of the method used, it's important to consider the presentation of your lure or bait.

A few simple rules to remember about your presentation are: First you must get the fish's attention; and second, your presentation should cause the fish to strike.

The following pages cover various ways to accomplish both. Included in this chapter are tips on presenting spoons, spinners, spinner/buzzbaits, jigs, plastic worms, and additional techniques to improve your presentation skills. If you practice some of the ideas shown in this chapter, they should help you to catch more fish.

SPINNER/BUZZBAIT PRESENTATION TIPS

Spinnerbaits and Buzzbaits are one of the most popular lures used today. They come in a large variety of configurations and almost anyone can fish them effectively. The following are a few tips on how to use them.

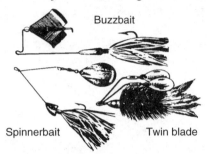

Buzzbait

Spinnerbait   Twin blade

BUMPING OR CONTACT RETRIEVE

Spinnerbaits are best used as contact lures. They should be bumped against some form of structure such as weeds, reeds, docks, stumps, logs, or submerged trees, using a slow to medium retrieve.

FLUTTER RETRIEVE

The flutter retrieve should be used when fishing steep banks, ledges, or dropoffs. After you make your cast, allow the lure to sink to the bottom, causing the blades to rotate (flutter) as the bait sinks. When it hits bottom, raise and lower the rod tip slightly.

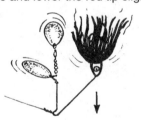

BUZZING RETRIEVE

When buzzing the surface using spinnerbaits, use the tandem blade version with Colorado blades because they run the shallowest. You can also use single blade versions or "Buzzbaits" that use either "Delta" or "Counter Turn Blades."

The retrieve should be fast and started as soon as the lure hits the water. The action of the blades should create a surface disturbance (surface bulge) as the lure is retrieved.

CRAWL/SLOW-ROLL RETRIEVE

With this retrieve, you creep or crawl the lure over timber, brush, or open water using a very slow retrieve. Tandem version spinnerbaits work best, and the retrieve should be just fast enough to make the blades turn.

CRANKBAIT PRESENTATION TIPS

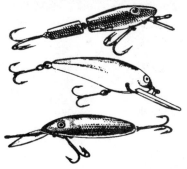

Lures called "Crankbaits" include swimming, wiggling, or wobbling plugs. Vast assortments of these types of plugs are available in today's marketplace in a variety of shapes, sink rates, sizes, and so forth. Usually, they are fished by casting them out, allowing them to sink, and then cranking them in. The following are a few tips on how to improve the presentation of these types of lures.

STOP AND GO RETRIEVE

Cast out the lure, start reeling rapidly for a short distance, and then stop. Lures that float will rise slowly , and suspending lures will remain at the same depth. Then start repeating the rapid reeling and stopping until you bring the lure in.

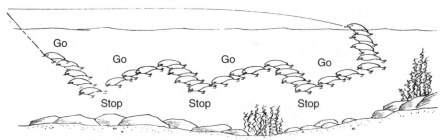

BOTTOM BUMPING RETRIEVE

Bottom bumping can be effective in both deep or shallow water. With this technique, the crankbait is jerked along the bottom kicking up silt as it runs erratically. When using this retrieve, make sure the lure dives deeper than the water depth you're fishing.

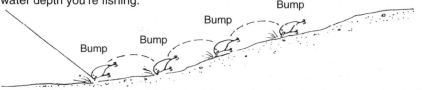

RIPPING RETRIEVE

With this technique, get the lure to the desired depth and then pull back on the rod with a short jerking action, causing the lure to dart quickly and erratically. Keep a taut line during the retrieve repeating the rod action.

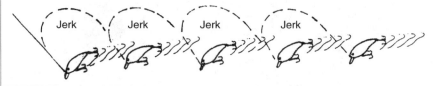

TOP-WATER LURE PRESENTATION TIPS

Top-water lures are basically considered lures which float on the surface or just below the surface. The different types include chuggers, poppers, stick baits, propbaits, minnow baits, and wobblers.

Many of them have some form of action when retrieved over the water surface; however, some of them require a fishermen's skill to add the action necessary to catch fish. The following are a few tips on working surface or topwater lures.

STOP AND GO RETRIEVE

When using surface lures, regardless of the type, try the following. After you cast, allow the lure to lay motionless for a while, and then start reeling in.

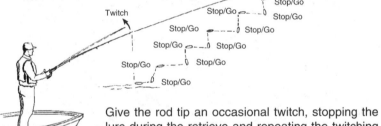

Give the rod tip an occasional twitch, stopping the lure during the retrieve and repeating the twitching action when you resume reeling.

JERK RETRIEVE

This retrieve should be used with stick baits, which for the most part have little or no action at all. It can also be applied to any of the other types of surface lures to enhance their built-in action.

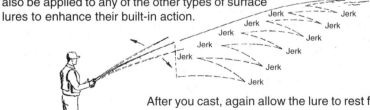

After you cast, again allow the lure to rest for a short period of time. Start reeling and give the lure an occasional short jerk with the tip of the rod during the retrieve. The jerk can be from side to side changing the lures direction.

PLASTIC WORM PRESENTATION TIPS

The following illustrations show a few of the more frequently used methods to retrieve a plastic worm, which have proven to be successful.

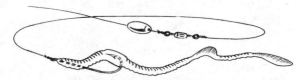

BOTTOM-BOUNCING OR HOPPING PRESENTATION

After you make your cast, allow the worm to fall on a tight line. After it hits the bottom, raise the rod tip slightly (a few inches) lifting the worm forward and then letting it hit the bottom again. Repeat the process over and over until the retrieve is completed.

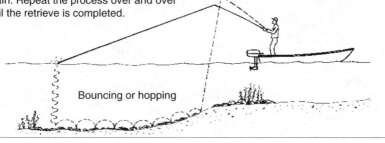

Bouncing or hopping

SWIMMING PRESENTATION

After the cast, keep a taut line and allow the worm to hit bottom. Using a slow and steady retrieve, bring the worm in while keeping it parallel to the bottom. Use a smooth level motion to give the worm the swimming effect.

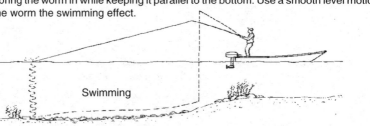

Swimming

COMBINATION PRESENTATION

After the cast, again keep a taut line and allow the worm to hit bottom. Start the retrieve using the bottom-bouncing or hopping method. Hop the worm a couple of times and then pause and switch to the slow swimming retrieve for a short period of time. Keep repeating and switching from the hopping to the swimming method as you bring the worm in.

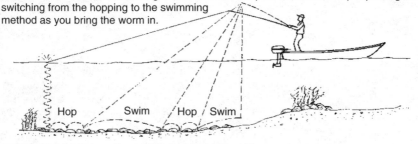

Hop   Swim   Hop Swim

SPOON PRESENTATION TIPS

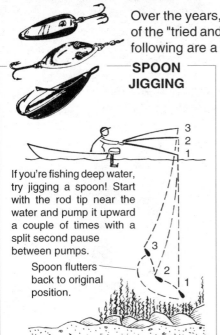

Over the years, spoon fishing has been ranked as one of the "tried and proven" methods for catching fish. The following are a few tips on presenting spoons.

SPOON JIGGING

If you're fishing deep water, try jigging a spoon! Start with the rod tip near the water and pump it upward a couple of times with a split second pause between pumps.

Spoon flutters back to original position.

COUNT DOWN RETRIEVE

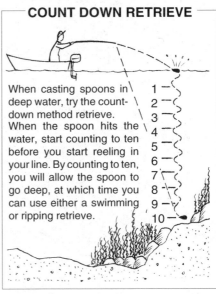

When casting spoons in deep water, try the count-down method retrieve. When the spoon hits the water, start counting to ten before you start reeling in your line. By counting to ten, you will allow the spoon to go deep, at which time you can use either a swimming or ripping retrieve.

1
2
3
4
5
6
7
8
9
10

SWIMMING A SPOON
Cold Water/Cold Weather Conditions

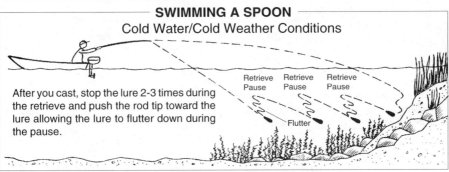

After you cast, stop the lure 2-3 times during the retrieve and push the rod tip toward the lure allowing the lure to flutter down during the pause.

Retrieve Pause   Retrieve Pause   Retrieve Pause

Flutter

RIPPING A SPOON
Warm Water/Warm Weather Conditions

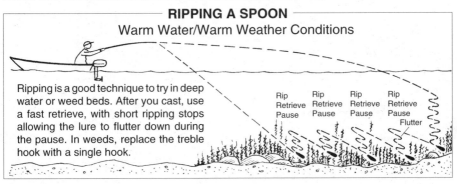

Ripping is a good technique to try in deep water or weed beds. After you cast, use a fast retrieve, with short ripping stops allowing the lure to flutter down during the pause. In weeds, replace the treble hook with a single hook.

Rip Retrieve Pause   Rip Retrieve Pause   Rip Retrieve Pause   Rip Retrieve Pause

Flutter

SPINNER PRESENTATION TIPS

Using spinners can be effective in many different fishing situations. They can be used when trolling, casting, or jigging.

Spinners are designed to create a flash and give a vibration sound when retrieved, attracting fish by sight and sound. The following are a few suggestions and tips on how to use them.

SPINNER SELECTION

Spinner selection should be based on angling conditions and the type of quarry you are after. The size of the spinner should be appropriate to the size of your quarry. They can be dressed with fur, feathers, or be just a plain hook type.

One thing to consider during your selection is the different blade sizes and shapes. Different blade shapes and sizes affect the rotational speed and the angle at which the blade rotates. Blade shapes also affect how the spinner should be retrieved. The larger blades like the Colorado work well with a fast retrieve, while the Indiana and willow leaf blades require a slower retrieve.

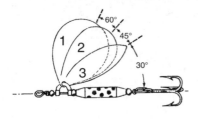

BLADE TYPES

1-Colorado   2-Indiana   3-Willow leaf

FAN CASTING

When using spinners, cover as much water as possible by fan casting a location prior to moving to another spot. To fan cast, keep casting and retrieving the lure either clockwise or counter clockwise in short increments as shown in the following illustration.

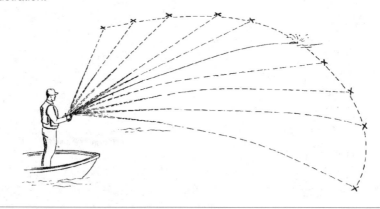

JIG PRESENTATION TIPS

The manner used to retrieve a jig presentation can be the difference between filling a stringer or going home empty-handed. Although there are no limits as to the number of jig movements a fisherman can use, the following illustrations show a few of the more frequently used methods that have proven to be successful.

BOTTOM-BOUNCING OR HOPPING PRESENTATION

After you make your cast, allow the jig to fall on a tight line. After it hits the bottom, raise the rod tip slightly (a few inches) lifting the jig forward and then letting it hit the bottom again. Repeat the process over and over until the retrieve is completed.

Bouncing or Hopping

SWIMMING PRESENTATION

After the cast, keep a taut line and allow the jig to hit bottom. Using a slow and steady retrieve, bring the jig in while keeping it parallel to the bottom. Use a smooth level motion to give the jig the swimming effect.

Swimming

COMBINATION PRESENTATION

After the cast, again keep a taut line and allow the jig to hit bottom. Start the retrieve using the bottom-bouncing or hopping method. Hop the jig a couple of times and then pause and switch to the slow swimming retrieve for a short period of time. Keep repeating and switching from the hopping to the swimming method as you bring the jig in.

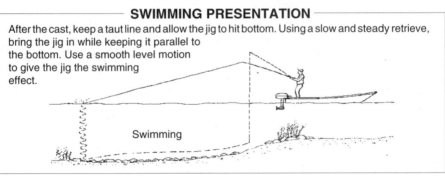

Hop   Swim   Hop   Swim

JIG TIPS-PRESENTATION

SIX IMPORTANT JIGGING TIPS

1. Become a line watcher. Any movement can be a strike or a pick-up. When it happens, set the hook.

2. Don't use snaps or swivels. Tie your line directly to the jig.

3. Use light line. Four-to-six-pound test line improves the action and gives you a better sense of feel.

4. Experiment with your retrieve. Vary the retrieves. Try swimming, bouncing, ripping, or combinations.

5. Be alert. Many hits occur on the drop or fall of the jig.

6. Try different jig sizes, styles, colors, weights, and dressings (including live baits).

BEST JIG DRESSINGS
COLD WATER CONDITIONS

Dressing: Marabou feathers
Presentation: Slow retrieve
Action: Pulsing reaction to slightest movement

Dressing: Marabou feathers with Nylon or pork rind strip
Presentation: Medium retrieve
Action: Pulsating feathers with vibrating tail

WARM WATER CONDITIONS

Dressing: Sassy shad or split tailgrub
Presentation: Slow retrieve
Action: Tails move with slight water pressure

Dressing: Curly tailed twisters
Presentation: Fast retrieve
Action: Vibrating tail

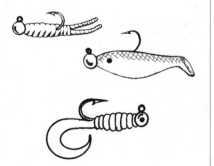

JIG TYPES

Jigs are the most popular lure type used today. They are no more than a weighted hook that can be dressed in a variety of ways. They are used for most any species of fish both in fresh or salt water. They are a very versatile lure that can be used during any season of the year. They can be fished tipped with live bait, plain with live or artifical bait, or dressed with feathers or other types of materials.

The shape of the head and the dressing are the determining factors that affect the sink rate, their effectivness and snag resistance.

The following chart illustrates the various types of jigs available and their recommended applications.

JIG STYLE	DESCRIPTION/CAPABILITY
FLATHEAD	Flathead jigs have a wide base and are very water resistant, making them slow sinkers. They should be used with a swimming retrieve when you are fishing for suspended fish.
ROUNDHEAD	Roundhead jigs have a fast sink rate. They are very effective in fast moving waters, and can be hopped, dragged, or swum. They are the most popular jig used today.
STAND-UP	Stand-up jigs have a flat base and are also very water resistant, making them slow sinkers. The flat base causes the hook to stand up, keeping the bait just above the bottom. They are very productive when fished through weed beds.
ARROWHEAD	Arrowhead jigs have a flat tapered head giving them a bulky apperance. They are fast sinkers and should be used to fish rocky areas.
BANANA	Banana jigs have a shape that resembles a fish. They are more snag resistant than most jigs, and the weight forward gives them a nose-diving effect when jigged.

JIG TIPS

JIG TYPES

JIG STYLE	DESCRIPTION/CAPABILITY
SPEARHEAD	Spearhead jigs have a shape that gives them a low water resistance. They should be used below dams and other turbulent areas.
FOOTBALL	Football jigs have a head shape that prevents them from tipping onto their sides when they rest on the bottom. They have a fast sink rate and can be hopped, dragged, or swum.
ERIE	Erie jigs are center-balanced jigs similar to the stand-up jig. The base causes the hook to stand up at a 45° angle, keeping the bait just above the bottom.
SHAD DART	Shad dart jigs have a slant-faced, tapered head, which makes them very water resistant. The slant-face adds action to the dressing when retrieved.
FLIPPING	Flipping jigs have a wide base and are very water resistant, making them slow sinkers and an excellent choice for ripping through weed beds. They should be used when bass fishing in heavy cover.
GLIDER	Glider jigs give the dressing a tipsy, back-and-forth motion when jigged. They should be used with a swimming retrieve, or they also can be used for bottom bouncing.
WORMING	Worming jigs are designed for plastic worm presentations. The barb on the jig head prevents the worm from slipping after it is attached, and also makes the presentation more snag resistant.

FLIPPING PRESENTATION

Flipping is a method of presenting lures, jigs, or baits into difficult locations in shallow waters such as weed beds, around piers, under docks, or over hanging brush. It's an excellent way to fish those hard to get spots that may be holding lunker bass or pike. Here's how to do it!

STEP 1

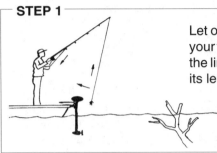

Let out the amount of line needed to reach your target area. With your free hand, grasp the line and pull back on the line about half its length while raising the rod tip.

Swing your lure, jig or bait under the rod toward you creating a pendulum effect.

STEP 2

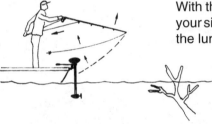

With the line in your hand behind you or to your side, start lowering the rod tip and get the lure swinging under the rod.

Lowering the rod tip will allow the lure, jig, or bait to swing further back and also gets the rod ready for the flip.

STEP 3

When the lure, jig, or bait starts forward, begin raise the rod tip and move your rod hand forward toward the target area to increase the speed of the swing.

At the end of the swing, give the rod a gentle flip and allow the line to slip through your fingers toward the target.

STEP 4

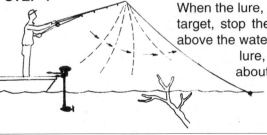

When the lure, jig, or bait approaches the target, stop the line with your hand just above the water. With a little practice the lure, jig, or bait can be stopped about one inch above the water allowing it to slip into the water with hardly a ripple.

MISCELLANEOUS PRESENTATION TIPS

NIGHT FISHING WITH SURFACE LURES

Surface lures that produce a constant noise when retrieved across the surface are excellent for night fishing. Most species can detect the sound and easily find the offering.

NIGHT FISHING MISDIRECTED CASTS

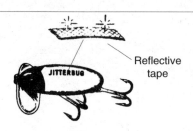

Reflective tape

A small piece of reflective tape added to your lure can be a big help in locating a misdirected cast that ends up in shoreside brush.

BUSHWACKER

Predators attack one victim at a time. They select victims that are apart from the school, isolated, disabled, or look different. Always fish the edges of feeding baitfish or make your presentation into the school and then retrieve away from it.

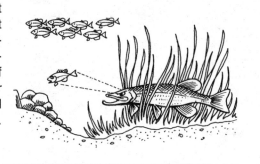

TROLLING SPOONS

Here's a trick to try that will elimate most hang-ups when you're trolling close to the bottom. Snip off the lower hook on the treble that's on the spoon or replace it with a double hook. In either case, the remaining hooks will ride point up, making the spoon less likely to snag the bottom.

TROUT PRESENTATION METHODS

Based on past surveys conducted over a three-year period, the following fishing methods were the most productive for taking trout.

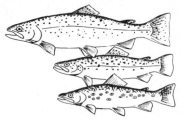
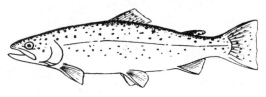

FISHING METHOD USED	TROUT SPECIES			
	Rainbow	Brown	Brook	Steelhead
Spinning	33%	42%	42%	26%
Spincasting	19%	13%	24%	15%
Still Fishing	17%	13%	11%	9%
Trolling	10%	13%	2%	13%
Baitcasting	9%	11%	8%	24%
Flyfishing	9%	4%	8%	8%
Ice Fishing	2%		2%	

TROUT ACTIVITY AND WATER TEMPERATURE

The following information is based on the general accepted temperature ranges for most trout.

WATER TEMPERATURE	FISH ACTIVITY/ LOCATION	SUGGESTED OFFERINGS
Freezing to 40°	Inactive/Very deep	Live baits
40° to 50°	Passive/Deep or warmer shallows	Live baits, Spoons, Spinners, Nymphs, Streamer flies
50° to 60°	Active/Near surface	Wet flies, Streamers, Nymphs, Spoons, Spinners
60° to 70°	Very active/Near Surface	Dry or wet flies, Streamers, Nymphs, Spoons, Spinners
70° to 80°	Active to passive/ Deep or undercuts	Live baits, Streamers, Nymphs, Spoons, Spinners
80° and higher	Inactive/Very Deep	Live Baits

GENERAL PRESENTATION TIPS

In order to catch fish with consistency, presentation can be a key factor to success. Using the proper fishing method and equipment, and knowing and understanding how the seasonal cycles (temperatures), water clarity, and other conditions affect fish, can be vitally important when presenting your bait or lure. Lure or bait selections used in the spring may not work in the summer or fall months and visa versa. You must be versatile in your selections as the seasons change. The following are a few tips to consider during the various seasonal changes when making your presentations.

GENERAL RULES

■ EQUIPMENT
Be line conscious.
Match the line and weights you use to the bait you use.

The fishing method and the equipment you use and how it's rigged must be considered during the presentation of your lure or bait. One of the key factors to a good presentation is the line you use to deliver your offering. Always use the lightest line possible in any given situation. Use a limp, soft line in deep waters where there are few obstructions, and a more durable stiff line when fishing weeds or dense cover. Also use the minimal amount of weight (sinkers) when bait fishing, as well as smaller and lighter hooks, bobbers, and so forth.

■ WATER TEMPERATURE
Be conscious of water temperatures.
Match your bait or lure to the conditions, and how you retrieve them.

During the spring, when the water temperature is extremely cold, small lures or baits work the best using a slow retrieve. In the summer months, use medium-size baits or lures with a moderate to fast retrieve. And in the fall, use larger baits and lures with a moderate to slow retrieve.

■ WATER CLARITY
Be conscious of the water clarity.
Match the lure to the color of the water.

When fishing clear waters, sneak up on the fish. When shore fishing, walk or wade softly to the likely spots. When you're fishing from a boat, use an electric motor or the wind to drift up to the area you want to fish. Explore fish holding edges like submerged logs, weedlines, piers, and moored boats.

As a rule, the clearer the water, colored lures like white, black, red, blue, or nickel plated work the best. In dark-colored water, fluorescent colors like purple, chartreuse, orange, and green are productive. On overcast days or at night, in water that has medium charity, use yellow, lime green, or orange lures, and in murky water with bright sunlight, chartreuse-colored lures are dynamite.

90

CHAPTER
5

FLY FISHING

Fly Fishing Tips

Fly fishing is considered one of the oldest and purest forms of fishing. It is a slow, artful, and relaxing way to fill a stringer once you learn the simple basics. In recent years, it has experienced a tremendous resurgence as more anglers discover how simple it is to learn, and how effective it is for catching fish.

This chapter is devoted to tips, tricks, and techniques on how to improve your fly fishing ability. It offers suggestions on presentation, equipment selection, equipment care, and fly selection, as well as tips on rigging your equipment.

EQUIPMENT SELECTION BY SPECIES

The following chart lists rods, reels, lines, and leader selections for specific game fish species.

The listings are only recommendations based on what the average fly fisherman uses today. When purchasing equipment, use the chart as a guide to help you make the right selection.

SPECIES	ROD	REEL	LINE	LEADER
PANFISH	7 to 8-1/2 ft.	3" to 3-1/2" Diameter	#4 or #6 Floating or #5,6, or 7 Sinking	3 to 4 lb.
BASS	7-1/2 to 9 ft.	3-1/4" to 4" Diameter	#6 to #8 Wt. forward	6 to 8 lb.
PIKE/MUSKIE	9 to 9-1/2 ft.	4" Diameter with adj. drag	#9 Wt. forward	10 to 12 lb.
TROUT	7 to 9 ft.	3" to 3-1/2" Diameter	#4 to #8 Double taper	2 to 6 lb.
SALMON	8 to 9-1/2 ft.	4" Diameter with adj. drag	#9 Wt. forward	10 to 12 lb.

TIPS ON FLY ROD SELECTION

ROD SELECTION FACTORS

In selecting a rod, consider its weight, strength, sensitivity, and power. These are the factors necessary to make the right choice. However, the most important factor of all is how it feels in your hand.

BAMBOO, FIBERGLASS, OR GRAPHITE?

The material the rod is made of is a personal choice. The following information lists some of the advantages and disadvantages of each type of material to help with your selection.

BAMBOO RODS

Bamboo rods have been around since the early 1700s and are a favorite with many anglers. They are lightweight and have excellent flexibility and sensitivity. The disadvantage of bamboo is the lack of toughness. They break easily and require a lot of care.

FIBERGLASS RODS

Fiberglass rods started to appear in the late 1940s and are still considered a first choice when selecting a rod. Fiberglass rods have excellent flexibility, power, and strength and are easy to cast with. The disadvantage of a fiberglass rod is its weight. When compared to both a bamboo or graphite rod, the weight can be a determining factor when you are making your selection.

GRAPHITE RODS

Graphite rods appeared in the 1970s and are the most common rods sold today. The advantage of a graphite rod over a fiberglass rod is its sensitivity and lightness. The disadvantages are that it's not as strong or tough as a fiberglass rod, and it's more difficult to cast with because of the stiffness of graphite.

Whether it's graphite, fiberglass, or bamboo, as a general rule, a 8-1/2' to 9-1/2 foot rod is considered the best choice for general fishing. The longer the rod the better, because the longer length will allow you more distance, longer line pickup, and better control. The following chart shows recommended rod selections by species.

SUGGESTED SELECTION BY SPECIES

PANFISH	BASS	PIKE/MUSKIE	TROUT	SALMON
7 to 8 -1/2 ft.	7 to 9 ft.	9 to 9-1/2 ft.	Average 7 to 9 ft. Steelheads 8 to 9-1/2 ft.	8 to 9-1/2 ft.

TIPS ON FLY LINE AND LEADER SELECTION

The secrets to getting the maximum casting performance from your fly fishing outfit are line balance, versatility, and skill. Skill can be obtained with practice and experience once you have selected the proper weight outfit for your fishing needs.

The most important thing to remember in fly fishing is that you cast the line and not the fly. That's why selecting the proper line is the key factor in fly fishing. The line that matches your fly rod is the key to how far and how easily you can cast your presentation.

Most rod manufacturers today recommend the proper line weight to use with their rods. A rod designed to use a 7 weight line, will balance with all 7 weight lines, regardless of the type of line or who manufactured the line. Whether it's floating, sinking, tapered, or weighted forward, if you use the wrong weight line, even with the most expensive rod, it won't perform properly. Once you have selected the proper weight line, versatility can be obtained by expanding your line selections to floating, sinking, weighted forward, and so forth to meet various fishing conditions so you can fish from top to bottom and anywhere in between.

The following chart is intended to help you make the proper choices when selecting your lines and leaders.

LINE/LEADER SELECTIONS			
Line Weight	Application	Presentation Size	Tapered Leaders
#3 and #4	Ultimate presentation delicacy for dry flies. Difficult to cast in wind conditions.	Patterns in sizes 14 to 28.	4X to 8X .017 Dia. Butt
#5	Slightly compromised presentation delicacy. Easier casting.	Sizes 12 to 22 dry flies, or small streamer patterns.	3X to 7X .019 Dia. Butt
#6 and #7	Midpoint of delicacy. All-purpose casting, first choice of most anglers.	Size 8 dry flies, small nymphs, bass flies, and small streamers.	0X to 5X .021 Dia. Butt
#8 and #9	Diminished delicacy. Power casting of wind resistant presentations.	Large bass bugs and streamers in sizes 3/0 to 4.	2X or longer .023 Dia. Butt
#10 thru #15	Distance casting of large wind resistant presentations.	Large flies and poppers in sizes #4/0 to 2.	0X or longer .025 Dia. Butt

TIPS ON FLY ROD RIGGING

TYPICAL FLY FISHING RIG

The following illustration shows some of the simpler knots to use when assembling a fly fishing outfit. See chapter 3 for alternative knots to use when attaching fly lines, leaders, and presentations.

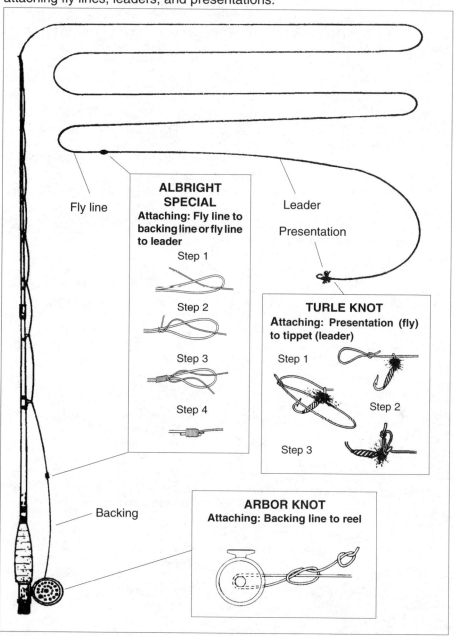

Fly line

Leader

Presentation

ALBRIGHT SPECIAL
Attaching: Fly line to backing line or fly line to leader

Step 1

Step 2

Step 3

Step 4

TURLE KNOT
Attaching: Presentation (fly) to tippet (leader)

Step 1

Step 2

Step 3

Backing

ARBOR KNOT
Attaching: Backing line to reel

WHAT PATTERN TO USE

PATTERN SELECTION BY SPECIES

The following chart lists fly pattern selections for specific game fish species, which for the most part have worked successfully when fished properly.

SPECIES		SUGGESTED PATTERNS	HOOK SIZE
PANFISH 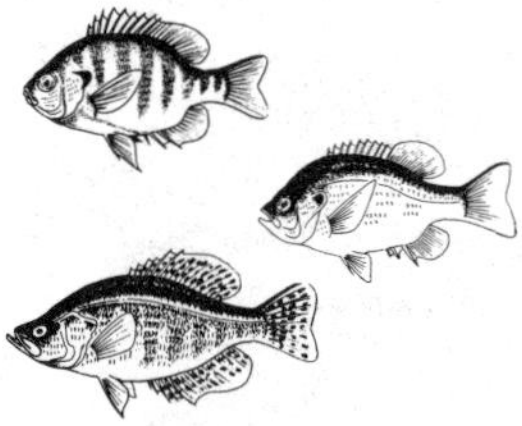	Bluegills Sunfish Crappies	■ Rubber spiders ■ Small wet flies ■ Small dry flies ■ Small streamers	#12 to #14
BASS 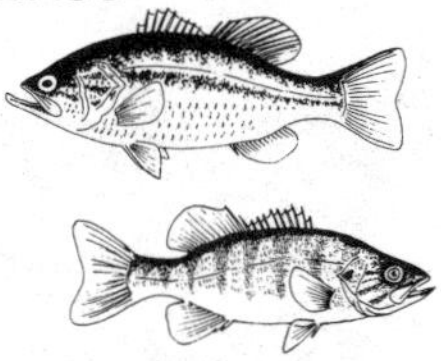	Largemouth Smallmouth	■ Poppers ■ Feathered minnows ■ Streamers ■ Grasshopper imitations ■ Hellgrammite imitations	#4 to #6
PIKE/MUSKIE 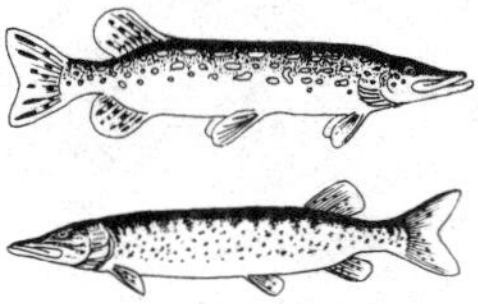	Northern Pike Muskellunge	■ Large saltwater streamers ■ Dalberg divers ■ Mega streamers	#1/0 to #3/0
TROUT 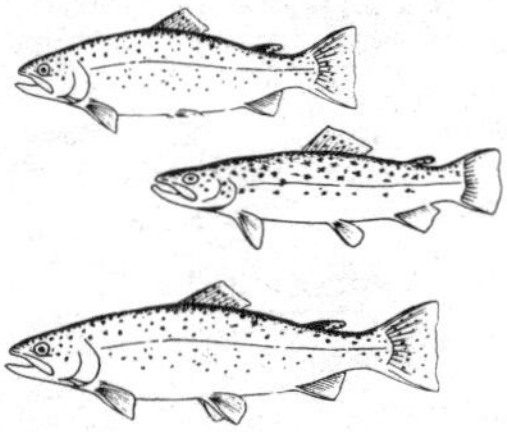	Rainbow Brown Steelhead	■ Dry flies ■ Wet flies ■ Nymphs ■ Streamers ■ Spawn egg imitations	#10 to #20
SALMON 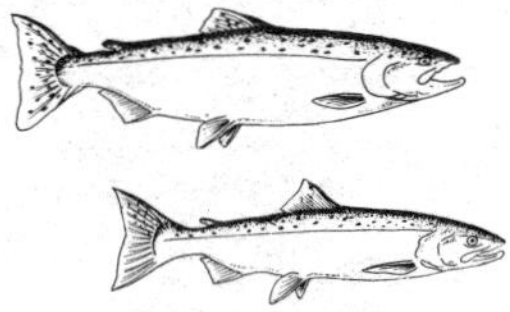	Chinook Coho	■ Dry flies ■ Wet flies ■ Streamers ■ Spawn egg imitations	#6 to #6/0

RECOMMENDED PANFISH PATTERNS

BLUEGILLS, SUNFISH, and CRAPPIES

The following examples are only a few of today's more effective patterns (sizes #12 to #14) to use when fly fishing for panfish.

- Small terrestrials
- Small wet flies
- Small dry flies
- Small nymphs

TERRESTRIALS

Ant Patterns
- Black ants
- Flying ants
- Red ants
- McMurray ants

Sponge spiders

Wooly worm patterns

Cricket patterns

Hopper patterns

WET FLIES
Assorted patterns

Wet Fly Patterns
- Leadwing Coachman
- Butcher
- Blue Zulu
- McGinty
- Black Gnat
- Adams
- Quill Gordan

CRUSTACEANS

Freshwater scud patterns

DRY FLIES
Assorted patterns

Fanwings   Midges   Mosquitos

Dry Fly Patterns
- Royal Coachman
- Adams
- Poly Quill Spinner
- Cahill
- Black Gnat
- Black Midge

Gnats

Spinners

NYMPHS

Prince Nymph   Peeking Caddis

Sparkle Larva   Zug Bug

RECOMMENDED BASS PATTERNS

LARGEMOUTH and SMALLMOUTH BASS

The following examples are only a few of today's more effective patterns (sizes #4 to #6) to use when fly fishing for bass.

- Poppers
- Feathered minnows
- Crustaceans
- Insect imitations
- Streamers
- Frogs and mice

POPPERS

Pencil popper patterns

Hair popper patterns

Cork popper patterns

INSECT IMITATIONS

Cricket patterns

Hopper patterns

Wooly worm patterns

FEATHERED MINNOWS

Zonker patterns

Sculpin patterns

Muddler patterns

STREAMERS
Assorted streamer patterns

Leech patterns

Wooly bugger patterns

Bait fish imitation patterns

CRUSTACEANS

Crayfish patterns

Scud patterns

FROGS and MICE

Hair mouse patterns

Hair frog patterns

NORTHERN PIKE and MUSKELLUNGE

The following examples are only a few of today's more effective patterns (sizes #1/0 to #3/0) to use when fly fishing for pike or muskie.

- Large saltwater/freshwater streamers
- Large poppers
- Large frog and mice patterns

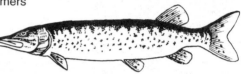

LARGE SALTWATER and FRESHWATER STREAMERS

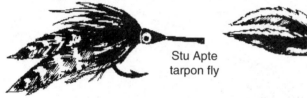

Stu Apte tarpon fly

Cockroach

Lefty's Deceiver

Large freshwater streamer patterns

LARGE POPPER PATTERNS

Cork popper patterns

Pencil popper patterns

LARGE FROG and MICE PATTERNS

Hair mouse patterns

Hair frog patterns

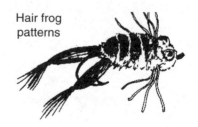

RECOMMENDED TROUT PATTERNS

RAINBOW, BROWN, and STEELHEAD TROUT

The following examples are only a few of today's more effective patterns (sizes #10 to #20) to use when fly fishing for trouth.

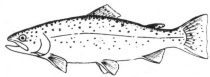

- Dry flies
- Wet flies
- Nymphs
- Streamers
- Spawn egg imitations
- Crustacean patterns

DRY FLIES
Assorted patterns

Fanwings   Midges   Mosquitos

Dry Fly Patterns
- Royal Coachman
- Adams
- Poly Quill Spinner
- Cahill
- Black Gnat
- Black Midge

Gnats

Spinners

NYMPHS
Assorted Patterns

Prince Nymph   Peeking Caddis

Sparkle Larva   Zug Bug

WET FLIES
Assorted patterns

Wet Fly Patterns
- Leadwing Coachman
- Butcher
- Blue Zulu
- McGinty
- Black Gnat
- Adams
- Quill Gordan

STREAMERS
Assorted streamer patterns

Leech patterns

Wooly bugger patterns

Bait fish imitation patterns

SPAWN EGG IMITATION PATTERNS

Single egg patterns   Egg sucking leech

CRUSTACEANS

Freshwater scud patterns

RECOMMENDED SALMON PATTERNS

CHINOOK and COHO SALMON

The following examples are only a few of today's more effective patterns (sizes #6 to #6/0) to use when fly fishing for salmon.

- Dry flies
- Hairwing salmon flies
- Streamers
- Bait fish imitations
- Spawn egg imitations

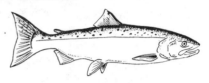

DRY FLIES
Assorted patterns

Humpy patterns

Henryville Special

Wulff patterns

HAIRWING SALMON FLIES
Assorted patterns

Skykomish Sunrise

Purple Peril

McCleod's Ugly

Green Butt Skunk

BAIT FISH IMITATIONS
Assorted patterns

Zonker patterns

Sculpin patterns

Muddler minnow patterns

STREAMERS
Assorted patterns

Silver Comet

Coho Streamer

Boss

Babine Special

SPAWN EGG IMITATIONS

Single egg patterns

Egg sucking leech

TANDEM FLY PRESENTATIONS

Tandem fly combinations are effective presentation methods to add to your fishing arsenal under difficult conditions when nothing else seems to work.

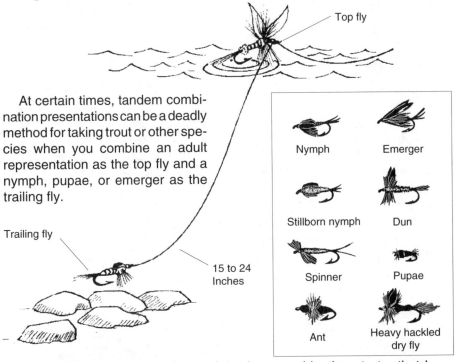

Top fly

At certain times, tandem combination presentations can be a deadly method for taking trout or other species when you combine an adult representation as the top fly and a nymph, pupae, or emerger as the trailing fly.

Trailing fly

15 to 24 Inches

Nymph

Emerger

Stillborn nymph

Dun

Spinner

Pupae

Ant

Heavy hackled dry fly

The following chart lists some of the best combinations to try that have proven to be very successful.

PATTERN SELECTIONS

MAYFLY COMBINATIONS

TOP FLY	TRAILING FLY
Mayfly nymph (unweighted)	Nymph (weighted)
Mayfly emerger	Nymph (weighted)
Mayfly stillborn nymph	Emerger
Mayfly stillborn nymph	Nymph (unweighted)
Mayfly dun	Nymph (weighted)
Mayfly dun	Emerger
Mayfly dun	Dun (smaller size)
Mayfly dun	Spinner
Mayfly spinner	Spinner (smaller size)

CADDIS COMBINATIONS

TOP FLY	TRAILING FLY
Caddis adult	Pupae
Caddis papae	Papae
Caddis adult	Adult

MIDGE COMBINATIONS

TOP FLY	TRAILING FLY
Midge papae	Midge pupae

TERRESTRIAL COMBINATIONS

TOP FLY	TRAILING FLY
Hopper	Ant (sinking)
Cricket	Ant (sinking)
Ant (winged)	Ant (sinking
Beetle	Jassid

STONEFLY COMBINATIONS

TOP FLY	TRAILING FLY
Stonefly adult	Nymph
Stonefly nymph	Nymph

ATTRACTOR PATTERN COMBINATIONS

TOP FLY	TRAILING FLY
Hairwing dry	Nymph
Irresistible	Ant (sinking)
Any heavy hackled dry fly	Wet fly (soft hackle pattern)

FLY CASTING TIPS

Like any sport, you must practice and work at fly fishing to become proficient. Once you've mastered the basic overhand cast in fly fishing, there will be situations that will require some additional casting skills during your fishing endeavors. The following pages show two casting techniques that will help make your fishing experience more enjoyable.

ROLL CAST

One of the important casts to learn in fly fishing is the roll cast. When stream, river, or shore fishing, many areas will be overgrown with trees, hampering your ability to use the overhand cast because of the limited space behind you. With the roll cast, the space problem can be solved because the line will not travel more than 10-12 inches behind you. The following illustrations and steps show how to execute a roll cast.

Step 1.
To begin, let out 15 feet of line in front of you. You can use a overhand cast in any open direction, or you can strip the line from the reel and shake it out through the rod tip.

Let out 15 feet of line

Hold and apply tension to line

Step 2.
Slowly bring the rod tip back (straight up) and over until your rod hand is at a point behind your eye and the rod is slightly over your shoulder and pause. Hold onto the line from the reel with your opposite hand applying tension to the line.

Bring rod tip back over your shoulder about 10 to 12 inches and slightly pause

Hold and apply tension to line

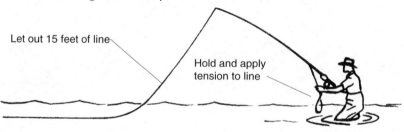

ROLL CAST-Continued

Step 3.

After the slight pause with the rod over your shoulder, start the forward downward stroke. It should be a strong, hard stroke with great force, causing the line in the air to pull the rest of the extended line off the water in a smooth fast-moving roll.

The forward movement of the rod is made by driving the rod downward with a stiff wrist and forearm action, causing the line to travel forward before the leader and presentation have left the water. The downward stroke should be completed when the rod tip is back at eye level.

Start forward downward stroke

Hold and apply tension to line

Step 4.

To get greater distance, as the rolling loop builds, release the line in the opposite hand, allowing the line to shoot out the slack as you would in the overhand cast.

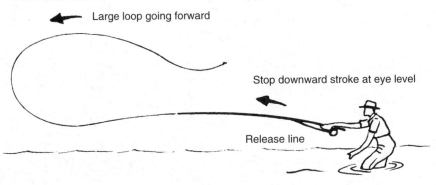

Large loop going forward

Stop downward stroke at eye level

Release line

A few important things to remember when practicing the roll cast are: Don't try it on dry land because it requires water-surface tension to complete, and also give the line a slight motion toward you when you start the forward cast.

In addition to learning the roll cast, another casting technique to learn is the power cast or double haul. The power cast or double haul is used for distance when you need a little more line to reach your target. The following illustrations and steps show how to execute the power cast.

POWER CAST

Once you have mastered the overhand cast, with a few additional gestures of your line hand, you will be able to gain greater casting distance by using the power cast or double haul casting technique.

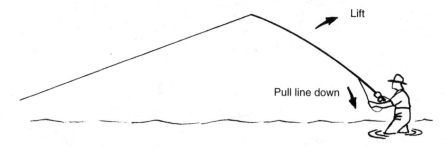

Step 1.

To begin the power cast, once you have your line out with your overhand cast, grab the line and pull down on it as you lift the rod during the backward movement. Lift the rod smoothly keeping a stiff wrist while pulling down on the line with your line hand.

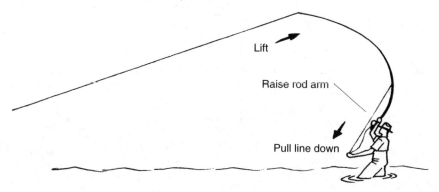

Step 2.

As the tension builds during the lift, accelerate your rod hand movement, raising your rod upward, and continue pulling down on the line with your line hand until both arms are fully extended in opposite directions.

POWER CAST-Continued

Step 3.

With the line behind you, brake with a slight pause while sliding the line upward with your line hand prior to starting the forward motion of the rod. Don't release the line in your line hand.

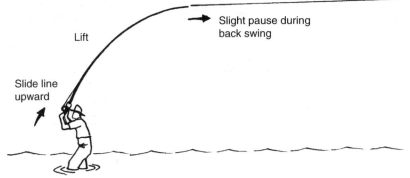

Lift

Slight pause during back swing

Slide line upward

Step 4.

Start the forward motion of the rod, pushing the rod forward smartly in a downward motion while pulling the line down again with your line hand as far as possible.

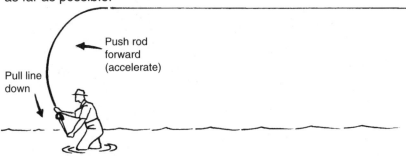

Push rod forward (accelerate)

Pull line down

Step 5.

Accelerate the downward push of the rod, stopping at eye level and release the line in your line hand. The additional tension of the push-pull technique with the line hand will cause the slack line to shoot forward giving you greater distance.

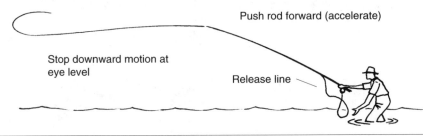

Push rod forward (accelerate)

Stop downward motion at eye level

Release line

PATTERN REPRESENTATIONS

PATTERN CATEGORIES

Most fly patterns used today, are representations of some sort of food that fish are accustomed to eating. Basically, they can be broken down into four groups: water insects, land insects, baitfish, and miscellaneous creatures. The following information describes what each group consists of and the types of patterns tied to represent them.

WATER INSECTS

Consisting of both dry and wet fly patterns that include representations of stone flies, caddis, mayflies, dragon flies, hellgrammites, and the various life stages of each, such as nymphs and emergers.

BAIT FISH

Consisting primarily of streamer patterns that include representations of minnows, sculpins, small panfish, and so forth.

LAND INSECTS

Consisting of both dry and wet fly patterns that are representative of grasshoppers, crickets, beetles, caterpillars, moths, ants, and so forth.

MISCELLANEOUS CREATURES

Consists of hair patterns, poppers, and most any other type of materials used to tie patterns. This is a catch-all category that includes representations of amphibians such as frogs, toads, tadpoles, newts; surface creatures such as mice and rats; crustaceans such as crayfish, scuds, and shrimp. It also includes leeches and most anything that doesn't fit into the other three categories.

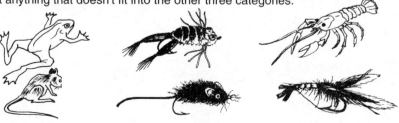

FLY LINE TIPS
The following are just a few tips on using and caring for your fly line.

■ Avoid exposing any fly line to insect repellents, gasoline, or other solvents. They will usually damage the line finish.

■ Make sure you use a tapered leader that has a butt end approaching the diameter of the fly line at the point of connection.

■ Select a line that matches your rod. Make sure the line brings out the proper action of your rod.

■ When putting on a new tapered line, trim the terminal end to match the diameter of your tapered leader.

■ Keep your line clean to improve its floating qualities.

■ Use braided nylon as backing; monofilament nylon is too elastic.

WADERS

Here's a tip to keep your waders or boots from getting a permanent crease or to help them dry out faster.

If you can find some large cardboard tubes like the ones used with new carpeting, save them and use them for your boots by cutting them to size and inserting them inside the boots.

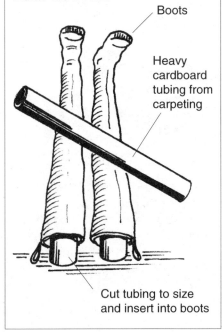

Boots

Heavy cardboard tubing from carpeting

Cut tubing to size and insert into boots

CREEL CARE

When using a creel to hold your fish, add some grass or leaves along with the fish. Also occasionally dip it in cold water to keep your fish fresh.

After you're done, remember to wash out the creel with a little baking soda, which will keep it sweet smelling and fresh.

FLY FISHING TIPS

STEAMED FLYS

If your favorite fly pattern gets matted or dirty, or the hackles need to be fluffed-up, hold it with a pair of forcepts over the steam from a boiling tea kettle. If the tea kettle steam doesn't work, use an oil can filled with water rather than the kettle for a real steam job.

STRIKE INDICATOR

Cement a piece of peacock herl or other water-resistant material to the splice where the leader meets the fly line. Even the lightest nibble or strike can be detected with this setup.

Peacock herl

NYMPH PRESENTATION

When using nymph patterns, attach a BB-size split shot fifteen inches above the fly to help take it down. Retreieve the nymph using quick short jerks to simulate the fast swimming action of a live nymph.

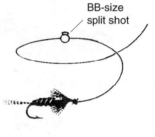

BB-size split shot

PIKE PATTERNS

If you have a chance to pick up some ultralarge streamers, especially the red and white ones used for tarpon fishing, give them a try at your favorite pike lake.

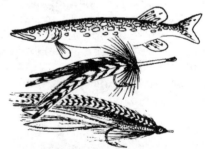

Northerns will grab a large fly faster than most famous pike-getter lures. If you can't find any to buy, try tying your own from the many pike patterns available today or create your own patterns.

There is nothing more satisfying than hooking a monster pike on something you created.

CHAPTER
6

FLY TYING

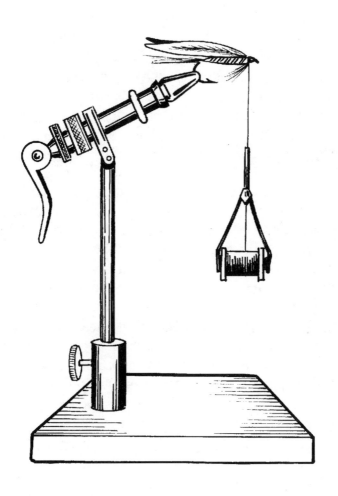

Fly Tying Tips

Nothing is more relaxing or satisfying than the ability to sit down at a vise and create your own lure or fly pattern that catches fish. Once you've accomplished this by learning the basics of fly tying, you're hooked forever, and the next step is to improve your newly acquired skill.

The following information contained in this chapter is intended to do just that—improve your skills. It covers many facets involved in fly tying such as collecting materials, dying materials, using new materials, and so forth. It also includes many short-cuts, tips, and tricks to make your fly tying more enjoyable.

Much of the information presented here came from experienced tiers, my own personal experience, and a multitude of other sources. I hope that some of the information presented here will be helpful regardless of whether you're an experienced tier or a novice.

AQUATIC INSECTS FISH FEED ON

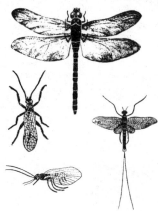

The most productive fly patterns are those that imitate or suggest a natural type of insect that fish feed on. Many insects lay their eggs in streams, rivers, ponds, and lakes; eggs emerge as nymphs or larva as part of their life cycle prior to reaching adulthood. Most of these insects go through a hatching process during a specific time of the year, at which time, their abundance causes feeding frenzies by all types of fish species. To the experienced fisherman, knowing or observing when the hatching process takes place, and having the ability to "match the hatch" with a fly that resembles the insect can produce wonderful results.

To be an expert fisherman or fly tier, you must have the fundamental knowledge of what these insects look like, and the various stages they go through in their life cycle. Once you gain that knowledge, you will be able to tie patterns that imitate or resemble the natural insects that will be productive during your fishing endeavors. The following pages and illustrations show the more common insects fish feed on.

May Flies *(Ephemeridae)*

The may flies are a favorite food for many fish. They are found near freshwater where they lay their eggs, which undergo metamorphic changes as they hatch and grow into adults. The nymph form of the mayflies can live for two to three years, while the adults live only a few hours to a day or two. The dun stage of the mayfly occurs when the nymph has developed wings and is ready to molt into the adult stage. At this time, fish start feeding on the nymphs as they begin to raise to the surface to hatch. There are many varieties of the mayfly, varying in colors, sizes and shapes, and providing a vast number of pattern possibilities for the fly tier.

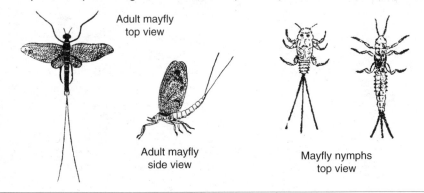

Adult mayfly
top view

Adult mayfly
side view

Mayfly nymphs
top view

AQUATIC INSECTS FISH FEED ON
Alder Flies *(Sialis Infumata)*

Alder flies look somewhat like the caddis fly. The adult is a land-flying insect that lives near water and lays its eggs on trees and shrubs that overhang or are close to the water. When the eggs hatch, the larvae crawl into the water, feeding on small water creatures until they near adulthood (pupal stage), at which time they crawl back onto the bank and bury themselves until they emerge as adults. Most fish feed on the larvae at the time when they are returning to the bank.

The American alder fly is nearly black in color, while the British alder is brownish in color. Adler patterns tied in the larva stage should be fished wet or half submerged for the best results.

Adult alder fly   Alder fly larva

Caddis Flies *(Trichoptera)*

The adult caddis fly lives on land, laying its eggs on water plants such as the sedges just above the water or under the surface. The larvae hatch from the eggs and build a case using plant material, bark, sand, or stones to live in.

Adult caddis fly

After the larva is fully grown, it seals the case and goes into the pupal stage where it grows wings. When the wings are grown, it opens the case and swims to the surface to emerge as an adult.

Caddis fly larva

Caddis flies emerge at night and can often be found in the larva stage during the early part of the trout season. Patterns can be tied in all stages including representations of the larvae in the case.

Larva in case

Crane Flies *(Diptera)*

Adult crane fly

Crane flies resemble mosquitoes, but they are much larger. They live in vegetation around water and are often called water spiders. The original spider patterns were made to imitate adult crane flies. Some species of crane flies form swarms over water like midges do during the mating process. They do lay their eggs in water; however, most patterns tied to represent the crane fly are the adult version rather than the larva stage.

AQUATIC INSECTS FISH FEED ON

Damsel and Dragon Flies *(Odonta)*

Both damsel and dragon flies are well known by most fishermen. They are insects that live around lakes, rivers, streams, and ponds and lay their eggs in water.

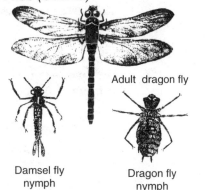

Adult dragon fly

They are a common sight seen hovering over the surface of the water most any time of day. Both nymphs and adult forms are eaten by most fish species, and a well-tied imitation of either the nymph form or an adult can be an excellent producer.

Damsel fly nymph

Dragon fly nymph

Stoneflies *(Plecoptera)*

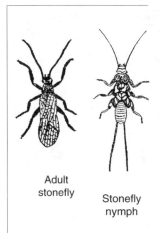

Adult stonefly

Stonefly nymph

Stoneflies are always found near fresh water on rocky shores of lakes or streams. They can be brown, black, gray, yellow, and sometimes green in color and have long antennae. The female deposits her eggs in the water; eggs separate and attach themselves to plants or rocks by a long thread.

The eggs hatch into the nymph stage and cling to the undersides of rocks or stones. The nymphs have two long tails at the ends of their bodies, and are carnivorous, eating other aquatic creatures. When the nymph matures, it crawls up on shore or a rock, and a wing adult emerges. Stone fly patterns are usually tied and fished wet style for the best results.

Midges, Mosquitoes, Gnats, Black Flies *(Odiptera)*

Midges, mosquitoes, gnats, and black flies are all found near water. These small insects lay their eggs in the water and undergo a complete metamorphosis.

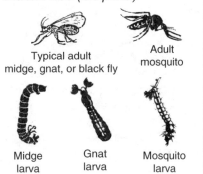

Typical adult midge, gnat, or black fly

Adult mosquito

The adult insects are often seen dancing in large numbers over ponds, lakes, and streams. Most patterns are tied as dry flies representing the adult insect. However, pupae patterns can also be very effective.

Midge larva

Gnat larva

Mosquito larva

115

AQUATIC INSECTS FISH FEED ON
WATER BEETLES

Imitation water beetles as a whole don't catch many fish. Very few patterns have been created to represent water beetles, which may be the reason why. At times, they can be very productive, depending on conditions and specific fish species that feed on them. Trout will eat water beetles during the early spring, prior to the time when other aquatic insects become active. The following are examples of the more common beetles found in ponds, lakes, rivers, and streams.

Water Beetles *(Hemiptera)*

Great Diving Beetle

Great diving beetles are approximately an inch long and are olive brown in color. They eat other aquatic animals like tadpoles, snails, and insects. The larva of the diving beetle is considered one of the most ferocious animals living in fresh water.

Great diving beetle larva

Adult great diving beetle

Silver Water Beetle

The silver water beetle resembles the great diving beetle, except for its silvery appearance. It looks silver because it carries a reservoir of air around its body, giving it a silver cast. It is larger than the great diving beetle, attaining a length of more than an inch. It also feeds on other aquatic creatures.

Silver water beetle larva

Adult silver water beetle

Water Boatman

Water boatmen are small water beetles that are usually less than an inch long. They are also called backswimmers, because some varieties swim on their backs. The water boatman lays its eggs on floating weeds; eggs are harvested and sold as aquarium fish food.

Water boatman larva

Adult water boatman

POPPER BODY PLUG TOOLS

Many articles have been written on how to make poppers using either cork bodies or beach sandals (tongs). All of them require a lot of cutting, shaping, and sanding to form the bodies before applying them to the hook. For most tiers, it's a time-consuming and sometimes cumbersome method, which, for the most part, discourages the tier, because the end results leave a lot to be desired.

George Cik, from the "Chicago Fly Fishers" developed the following procedure for making and shaping popper bodies. It's simple and effective with the end result being a perfectly shaped popper body.

BODY PLUG TOOLS

The first thing George did, was to make a few tools to make the plugs from either cork or sandal material. The tools can be used in either a punch press or an electric hand drill or in the worst case, your bare hand. The following illustrations show how easily they can be made.

Step 1.

For assorted size plugs up to 3/8" diameter, all you need to do is to get a few pieces of various diameter tube (approximately 4" long) and sharpen the edges at one end with a file or grinder. These can be used in a punch press or a hand drill, which have a chuck that will take a 3/8" diameter. Also grind out a slot in the side of each tube as shown (for plug removal) and drill a hole through both walls for a hand grip. The hand grip for the hole can be a nail or a piece of metal rod, and the hole diameter should be slightly larger than the diameter of the nail or rod.

Note: Skip the hand grip if you use a hand drill or punch press.

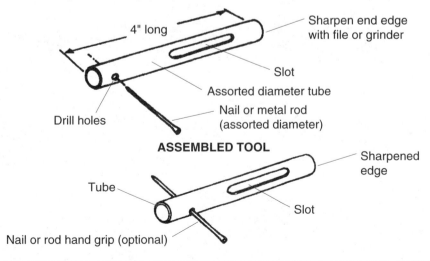

117

POPPER BODY PLUG TOOLS (continued)

 For plugs with a larger diameter than 3/8", you can make the following tools that will also fit the chuck in your punch press or hand drill.

Note: If you're going to make your plugs by hand, disregard this step and use step 1.

--- **BODY PLUG TOOLS** ---

Step 2.
Take a piece of 4" long tube with a 1/2" or 5/8" diameter and sharpen one end the same as in step 1. Also grind out the slot in the side of the tube as shown in the drawing.

Next, find a bolt with a hex head that will slip into the inside diameter of the tube.

■ 1/2" Diameter Tube: Use a 1/4-20 x 1/2" Long, 7/16" Hex Head Bolt
■ 5/8" Diameter Tube: Use a 3/8-16 x 1/2" Long, 9/16" Hex Head Bolt

Slip the bolt head into the tube, and using a hammer, distort the tube wall around the hex head of the bolt until it is captivated.

Note: Try to keep the bolt centered in the tubing when you distort the walls. For additional strength, you can also add some solder inside the tubing around the hex head after it is captivated.

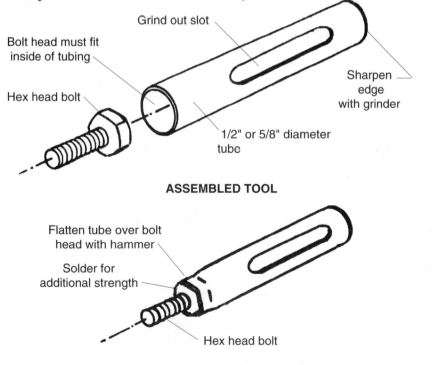

ASSEMBLED TOOL

POPPER BODY PLUG LATHE

The next thing George did after he made the plug tools was to build a simple lathe to shape the plugs. He built the lathe from a old sewing machine motor and a few miscellaneous items. The following illustrations show the complete unit and the various steps required to build your own. It really does a great job and is worth the time and effort to build.

REQUIRED MATERIALS

ITEM #	QTY.	DESCRIPTION
1	1	Sewing machine motor
2	1	Small drill chuck (mounted on motor)
3	A/R	Assorted wood screws with head removed (bits)
4	2	Large adjustable hose clamp (motor mounts)
5	4	Small wood screws or nails (hose clamp mounts)
6	1	2" X 6" X desired length wood block (base)
7	1	1" X 2" X 3" wood block (adjustable block)
8	1	Small finishing nail (retainer pin)
9	1	#10-32 X 2" long machine screw (adjustable block mounting)
10	1	Washer 3/16" diameter hole X .375 O.D. (adjustable block mounting)
11	1	Wing nut #10-32 (adjustable block mounting)
12	1	Foot switch with receptacle

A/R = As required

BODY PLUG LATHE

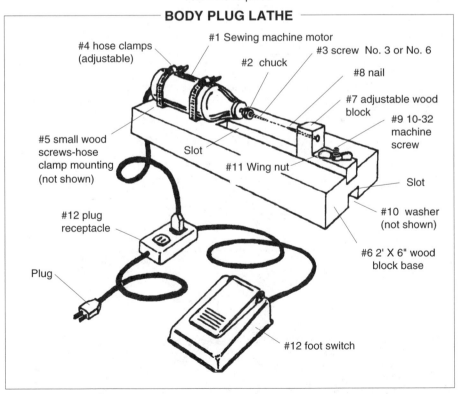

#4 hose clamps (adjustable)

#1 Sewing machine motor

#3 screw No. 3 or No. 6

#2 chuck

#8 nail

#7 adjustable wood block

#9 10-32 machine screw

#5 small wood screws-hose clamp mounting (not shown)

Slot

#11 Wing nut

Slot

#12 plug receptacle

#10 washer (not shown)

#6 2' X 6" wood block base

Plug

#12 foot switch

POPPER BODY PLUG LATHE (continued)
LATHE CONSTRUCTION AND ASSEMBLY

Step 1.

Start with a 2" X 6" piece of wood as your base and rout out a couple of slots 1" wide X 1/2" deep on both sides of the block as shown in the sketch. Next rout another slot 1/4" wide down the center of the first slots you made. This slot will be through the block.

WOOD BLOCK BASE

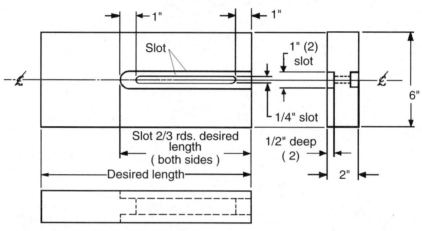

Step 2.

Next build the adjustable wood block as shown in the following sketch. Start with a 1" thick X 2" wide X 3" long block of wood and cut it per the dimensions in the sketch. Drill the 3/16" diameter holes.

ADJUSTABLE WOOD BLOCK

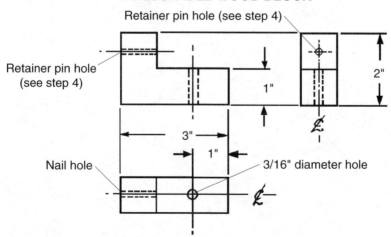

POPPER BODY PLUG LATHE (continued)
LATHE CONSTRUCTION AND ASSEMBLY

Step 3.

After you have completed the base and the adjustable block, mount the sewing machine motor to the base using a couple of adjustable hose clamps.

Note: Nail or screw the center of the hose clamps to the base before you wrap them around the motor. After the motor is mounted, insert and secure the screw bit into the chuck. The screw bit can be made from a #4 or a #8 wood screw by removing the screw head.

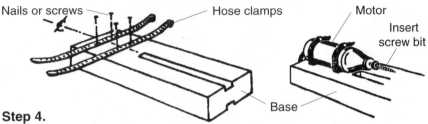

Step 4.

Next take the adjustable wood block and slide it down the slot to the screw bit to find the center location to drill the hole for the retainer pin. Once the center for the retainer pin has been located, drill a hole through the adjustable block as shown in the drawing.

Note: The hole diameter will be determined by the diameter of the nail used for the retainer pin.

Insert and epoxy the pin (nail) in the block.

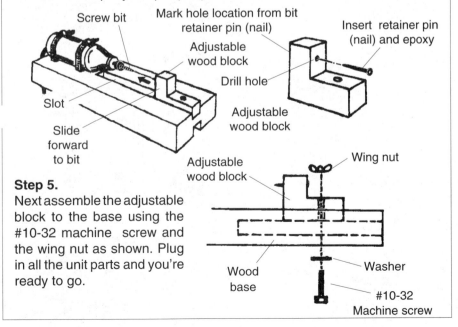

Step 5.

Next assemble the adjustable block to the base using the #10-32 machine screw and the wing nut as shown. Plug in all the unit parts and you're ready to go.

POPPER BODY PLUG LATHE (continued)
FOOTSWITCH AND RECEPTACLE WIRING

Once you have completed the construction and assembly of the lathe, the next step is to wire in the foot switch and the plug receptacle. The foot switch can be purchased at any sewing machine store and the receptacle at most hardware stores. You may find that some of the foot switches may include the receptacle already wired, in which case you can disregard this step.

The following illustration shows a bottom view of both the switch and the receptacle and how to wire them.

Note: After you have completed the wiring and plan to use your lathe, remember to use safety glasses when working on the plug bodies.

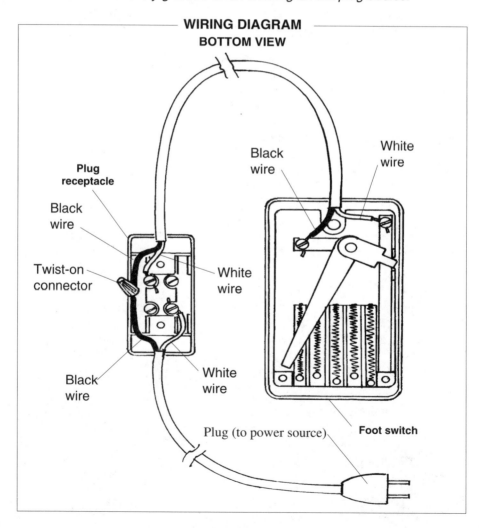

WIRING DIAGRAM
BOTTOM VIEW

Plug receptacle

Black wire

Twist-on connector

White wire

Black wire

White wire

Black wire

White wire

Plug (to power source)

Foot switch

POPPER BODIES

Step 1.

Punch or drill out an assortment of various size plugs from either cork or sandal material. After you punch or drill the material, remove the plugs from the tool, using the slot in the tool side to push out the plug.

Note: When using sandals, the more different colored sandals you have, the better the assortment of body plugs you can make.

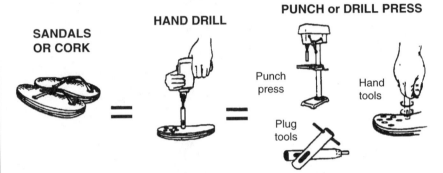

SANDALS OR CORK

HAND DRILL

PUNCH or DRILL PRESS

Punch press

Plug tools

Hand tools

Step 2.

Using the lathe, screw one of the plugs onto the screw bit.

Note: Be sure it's centered and bottomed on the bit.

Then slide the adjustable block forward until the retainer pin can be pushed into the center of the opposite end of the plug. Then secure the adjustable block with the wing nut.

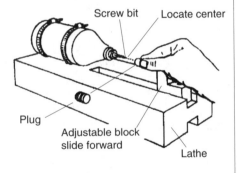

Screw bit   Locate center

Plug

Adjustable block slide forward

Lathe

Step 3.

Cut a few strips of sandpaper (assorted grits) about 1/2" wide.

Then starting with a slow speed using the foot switch, shape the plug into a bullet shape from the bit end forward with a coarse grade sandpaper strip. Once you have the desired rough shape, finish the sanding with a finer grit paper. Repeat steps 1 and 2 on all the plugs.

Note: For smaller plugs, you should use a smaller screw bit.

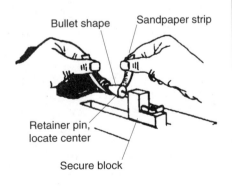

Bullet shape   Sandpaper strip

Retainer pin, locate center

Secure block

POPPER BODIES (continued)

Step 4.

After you shape the plug using the sandpaper, remove the retainer pin from the front end of the plug. Then using the blade of an X-acto knife, form a cup in the front end of the plug by placing the blade at an angle and using the tip to cut out the cup while the motor is running.

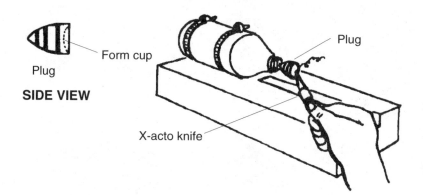

Plug

Form cup

Plug

SIDE VIEW

Plug

X-acto knife

Step 5.

After the cup is formed, remove the plug from the lathe, and using a razor blade or an X-acto hand saw, cut a slot in the bottom of the plug (halfway through the body) for the hook shank.

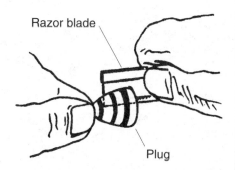

Razor blade

Plug

Step 6.

If you used sandal material for your popper body, for the most part, it's finished, or you can do the following.

If you have a Dremel tool, you can cut out a pair of eye sockets on each side of the plug to mount in a pair of doll eyes. The diameter of the eye sockets will depend on the size eyes you select. If you used cork material, all that's left is the painting to finish the popper body.

Cut slot halfway through plug (front to back)

Plug

Add eye sockets (optional)

SIDE VIEW

The following are a few tips on bleaching material and burning feathers.

BLEACHING MATERIALS

There are a few simple rules to remember when bleaching materials.

BLEACH SOLUTION

Don't use household bleach! Only use household bleach for burning or defluing feathers. The proper bleaching agent to use is hydrogen peroxide, a 20% volume mixture used full-strength.

Rule 1.

Never bleach feathers! Bleaching feathers destroys the texture of the fibers. The only time to use bleach on feathers is "burning" for spey fly patterns.

Rule 2.

Only bleach fur when the natural shade is unobtainable.

BLEACHING FURS

When bleaching furs, make it a practice to check them frequently. The length of time to leave the material in the bleach will depend on the type of fur it is and its original color. The time can vary from a few hours to a few days. Experiment by trying a little at a time until you learn from experience.

"BURNING" FEATHERS

The following process is used to deflue feathers for various patterns such as spey flies or quill gordons.

REQUIRED MATERIALS

- Any household bleach
- Baking soda

Step 1.
Dilute Clorox bleach by 50% with warm water.

Step 2.
Immerse materials into solution and swish around until the feathers pucker up (you can see the difference).

Step 3.
Watch the feathers closely until the desired effect is reached.

Step 4.
Remove the materials from the solution and soak them in a solution of baking soda and water to neutralize the bleach.

Step 5.
Remove from the baking soda solution, rinse in clean water, and allow materials to dry.

After you accumulate a vast collection of various tying materials, you may find that your collection doesn't include a specific color you may need for some of the patterns you would like to tie. To get the proper color, most tiers will dye their own materials to obtain the proper colors. The following are a few tips on how to dye materials.

DYEING PROCESS

Step 1.
Prepare the material for the dye bath.

A. Mix a solution of detergent (Woolite or any dishwashing detergent) and warm water.

B. Soak the materials in the solution to soften the fibers and to remove any grease, grim, or dirt. Soaking length of time will depend on the types of materials. The following is a general rule of thumb.
Necks, capes, and poultry feathers..............................2 hrs.
Duck, geese, or oily-feathered birds.........4 to 6 hrs.
Deer, elk, moose and Calf tails............................2 hrs.
Most other furs..................2 hrs.

C. After the soaking, rinse the materials clean by using lukewarm water.

Step 2.
Take an empty plastic milk bottle (gallon size) and cut off the top as shown in the following illustration.

Cut off top portion of bottle

Empty gallon milk bottle

Step 3.
Add your dye (package powder or liquid) into the bottle and add two teaspoons of Glacial Acetic Acid.

Step 4.
Turn on your water tap and let it run until the water is hot. When it's good and hot, fill the gallon with the hot water, mixing the dye. If you use powdered dye, give it a few stirs to dissolve the powder.

Step 5.
Place your presoaked materials into the dye bath and, using a stick, swish the materials around. Leave the materials in the dye bath until you obtain the desired color shade you want. The color shade will look darker while the materials are wet.

Note: Don't mix different materials in the dye bath. Dye unlike materials separately, such as poultry, deer, duck, geese, and so forth.

Step 6.
After you're done dying the materials, remove them from the dye bath and rinse them under cool running water until the water runs clean. Squeeze out any excess water (do not wring).

Step 7.
Place the dyed materials on newspaper, (skin side down or skin side to skin side) and allow them to dry. Occasionally fluff up the materials during the drying process.

STYROFOAM EYES

Here's a way to make some neat eyes for streamer patterns, and so forth. All you need is a piece of thin styrofoam, a single hole hand punch, a toothpick, and a small bottle of model-making paint.

HOW TO MAKE STYROFOAM EYES

Step 1.
Starting with a thin piece of styrofoam (coffee cups, egg cartons, and so forth) punch out as many circles as you need using a hand punch.
Note: You can purchase various hole size punches at most any office supply store for under a dollar.

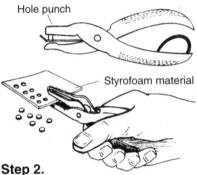

Hole punch

Styrofoam material

Step 2.
Next take a toothpick and cut off one of the tapered ends (the toothpick will be used as a paint brush).
Note: You can vary the size of the diameter you want to paint by cutting more than one toothpick at various points along the tapered end.

Step 3.
Using the toothpick, paint in the center of the eye on the styrofoam circle with model-making paint.
Note: It's a lot easier to paint if you stick the circles onto a piece of masking tape as shown below.

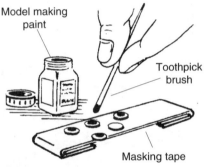

Model making paint

Toothpick brush

Masking tape

Step 4.
After the eyes are allowed to dry, they can be glued into position on your pattern. Use epoxy cement and cover the entire eye encasing it in the epoxy.

IMPORTANT: Don't use Pliobond or head cement, both of these cements will melt the styrofoam.

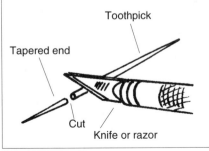

Toothpick

Tapered end

Cut

Knife or razor

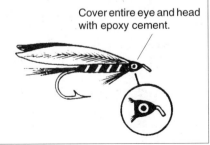

Cover entire eye and head with epoxy cement.

FEATHER NAMES AND LOCATIONS

The following chart shows the names and various locations of feathers found on bird wings referred to in many fly patterns.

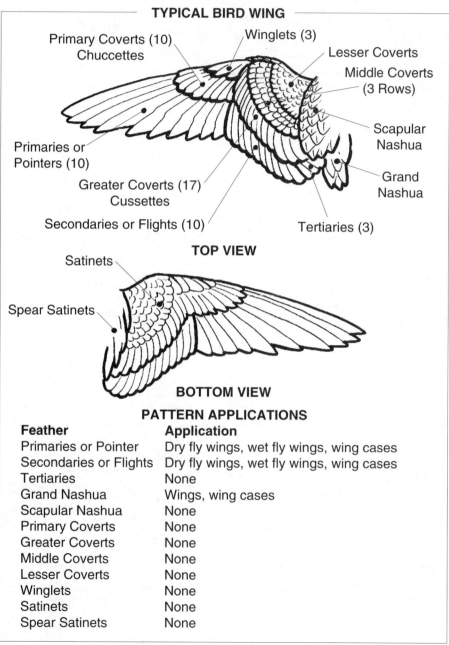

TYPICAL BIRD WING

Primary Coverts (10)
Chuccettes

Winglets (3)

Lesser Coverts

Middle Coverts (3 Rows)

Scapular Nashua

Primaries or Pointers (10)

Greater Coverts (17)
Cussettes

Grand Nashua

Secondaries or Flights (10)

Tertiaries (3)

TOP VIEW

Satinets

Spear Satinets

BOTTOM VIEW

PATTERN APPLICATIONS

Feather	Application
Primaries or Pointer	Dry fly wings, wet fly wings, wing cases
Secondaries or Flights	Dry fly wings, wet fly wings, wing cases
Tertiaries	None
Grand Nashua	Wings, wing cases
Scapular Nashua	None
Primary Coverts	None
Greater Coverts	None
Middle Coverts	None
Lesser Coverts	None
Winglets	None
Satinets	None
Spear Satinets	None

HOW TO MAKE SUBSTITUTE
JUNGLE COCK FEATHERS

Many patterns call for jungle cock feathers, which for the most part are used for cheeks or to represent the eyes in a pattern.

Jungle cock feathers are expensive and difficult to obtain because few supply houses carry them and most are brought in from out of the country from countries that still permit them to be exported.

As an alternative, the following is a simple procedure to apply to some of the feathers found on a common ringneck pheasant; these by no means replace the real thing, but for the most part can be used as a substitute.

Step 1.
Starting with the ringneck pheasant feather (neck, breast, or flank) strip off the fuzz at the base of the feather.

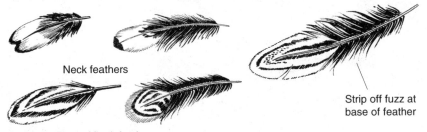

Neck feathers

Strip off fuzz at base of feather

Breast/ flank feathers

Step 2.
Using a small amount of clear silicone household sealer or bathtub calk, apply it to both sides of the feather.

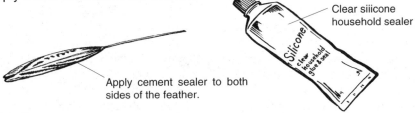

Clear silicone household sealer

Apply cement sealer to both sides of the feather.

Step 3.
Next pull the feather between your fingers, repeating the pulling process until the feather becomes slim and elongated. After you reach the desired shape, simply allow the silicone calk to dry and your feathers are ready to use.

Pull the feather between fingers

Finished substitute

PEACOCK EYED TAIL FEATHER TIPS

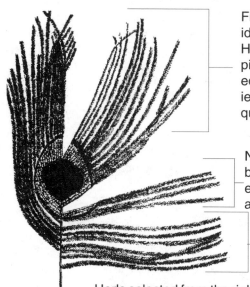

First, twelve to fourteen herls are ideal for "quill-bodied" patterns. Herl should be removed by stripping off fibers using a razor blade edge. To make light or dark bodies, select proper side of striped quill.

Next, four or five herls can also be used for "quill-bodies"; however, they are not as well suited as those above.

Next, eight to ten herls are most suitable for wrapping herl bodies such as those on coachman patterns.

Herls selected from the right side of the tail feather should be wrapped clockwise, while those selected from the left side should be wrapped counterclockwise. The results will give you a thicker, fuller body.

WEEDLESS PATTERNS

If you want your fly pattern (wets and streamers) to be just about weedless, dress the hook with the point up. The fly will ride through the water with the point up and will be less likly to snag weeds and so forth.

Conventional Method

Weedless Method

SINKING FLYS

If you want your wet fly patterns to sink without adding any additional weight, try using a heavier wire hook and quick saturating materials such as wools, hen feathers, and so forth. Avoid using any feathers from aquatic birds such as ducks, geese, and so on. The oils in aquatic birds repell water.

PANFISH POPPERS

You can make some dandy poppers from the rubber foam packed around fragile or electrical parts. It floats forever and can easily be dressed with rubber legs, resulting in excellent panfish lures.

CHAPTER
7
ICE FISHING

Ice Fishing Tips

If you're an ice fisherman, my hat goes off to you. It takes a special breed of fisherman to venture out into subzero temperatures, howling winds, and blowing snow to hard-water fish. Many fishermen are reluctant to try it because of these conditions; however, once you do, you will begin to understand the hours of enjoyment and success you can have fishing during the winter months.

The following pages in this chapter include a multitude of tips and tricks used to ice fish. Whether you use a tip-up, jig pole, or bobber fish, you may find some of the information presented here to be helpful in making your ice fishing experience more enjoyable.

ICE FISHING SAFETY TIPS

No one can stress enough the importance of safety precautions to take when ice fishing. Most ice fishing related accidents can be prevented by following proper safety precautions. The following are a few safety tips to remember when you're out hard-water fishing.

SAFETY TIPS

■ Never fish on ice less than three inches thick. Even three-inch thick ice can be dangerous on rivers, streams, or lakes where there is a current.

■ Be wary of newly formed ice in early winter or late season ice in March and April. Ice thickness can vary drastically during this time of the season.

■ Avoid areas where there are feeder creeks, springs, and dark, honeycombed, or porous ice.

■ If you fall through the ice, instead of trying to pull yourself out, try to swim out. By swimming, your body will rise up allowing you to get onto firm ice.

■ If you fall in, once you're out of the water, find shelter quickly.

■ Fish with a partner and carry a coil of strong rope with you. In case someone falls through, you can use the rope to rescue them.

■ When you put on your boots, loose lace them. If you go through the ice, you can kick them off, making it easier to tread water.

■ Watch out for frostbite. If necessary you should build a small fire on shore to warm up.

■ Know the symptoms of frostbite and hypothermia and what to do about them.

WHAT TO DO IF YOU FALL THROUGH

■ Stay calm; don't panic.

■ Use your legs and kick behind you to keep from being pulled under.

■ Try to stay in a horizontal position and extend yourself as far as possible onto the unbroken ice.

■ Work your way onto the unbroken ice while kicking your feet or trying to swim. If the ice breaks again, keep using this method until you reach firmer ice.

■ Once you're out, stay low and distribute your weight over as much surface area as possible. Move slowly.

■ Once on shore, get to a shelter as soon as possible. Treat yourself or get help to administer first aid for hypothermia.

HYPOTHERMIA SYMPTONS AND TREATMENT

Mild Hypothermia: Shivering, goose bumps, some loss of judgment, loss of motor skills, e.g., numb fingers, unable to zip up zipper. Body temperature is no less than 95°.

Treatment: Get to a shelter, remove wet clothes, sit by a fire, or take a warm shower or bath if available. Put on dry clothes and drink hot coffee, tea, or cocoa. Avoid alcoholic beverages.

Moderate Hypothermia: Violent shivering with possible muscular rigidity. Difficulty walking and talking. Body temperature 95° to 90°.

Treatment: Same as mild, with the addition of applying heat packs or hot water bottles to hands, feet, groin, neck, and armpits. Additional heat can be applied with body contact.

Severe Hypothermia: Shivering ceases, unable to walk, rigid, nonresponsive, white or pale gray skin, looks dead. Body temperature below 90°.

Treatment: Same as moderate, with the addition of wrapping victim in blanket and minimizing movement. Get help! Get to a hospital for rewarming under the supervision of a physician.

FROSTBITE SYMPTOMS AND TREATMENT

Symptoms: Pale areas of skin with pain in the tissues being affected, such as the chin, cheeks, ears, nose, fingers, toes, or any exposed flesh.

Treatment: Thaw affected areas with warm water or with hot, wet compresses. In severe cases, get help. Go to the nearest hospital.

HOMEMADE ICE CLAWS

Many ice fishermen venture out onto the ice without any type of safety device to use to save their lives if they accidently fall through. Even with a fellow angler to help them, they soon find out how tough it is to get out of the water with wet, heavy winter clothes and back onto safe ice.

The following simple tool, which can be made at home, is a device that can be used to pull yourself or your partner out of the water and back onto safe ice. It's simple to make and should be carried whenever you're out ice fishing.

MATERIALS REQUIRED

- 2 Six-inch long pieces of broomstick handle or 1-1/2" diameter wooden dowels
- 2 Sixteen-penny nails
- 1 Stout cord about three to four feet in length

Tie a stout cord about three to four feet in length to the wood handles.

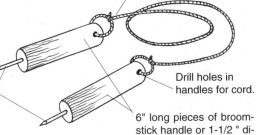

16-penny nails, hammered into the wood handles with about 2" protruding from the wood. Remove the heads and grind to a point.

Drill holes in handles for cord.

6" long pieces of broomstick handle or 1-1/2 " diameter wooden dowels

HOW TO USE THEM

1. Carry the ice claws slung around your neck so they are readily available.
2. If you go in, grab the claws with each hand and reach as far as possible from the hole and jam one of the claws into the ice.
3. Kick your feet as in swimming and reach beyond the first claw with your other hand and jam in the second claw.
4. Repeat the above procedure until you're on solid ice, then crawl or roll away from the hole. Don't stand up.
5. If your partner falls in, don't attempt to pull him or her out. Toss the claws and instruct him or her on how to use them.
6. Once you're out, seek shelter.

TRACTION

Take along a small bag of sand with you the next time you're out on the ice. Sprinkle the sand around your hole for a better footing. A slip on the ice may cause you to injure yourself or to go through the ice.

BOOTLACES

When you put on your boots, loose lace them. If you go through the ice, you can kick them off, making it easier to tread water.

Loose lace

ROD OR HAND-HELD LINE FISHING TIPS

The most common method used to ice fish is the rod or hand-held line method. This method consists of using various types of tackle such as a short light ice fishing pole (ice rod), a jigging pole, or a plain hand line. For most panfish, most anglers use a lightweight "panfish pole," while for perch, they use a deep-water rod (which is a stiffer version of the panfish pole) to fish deeper water. Both of these poles consist of a rod and a simple reel.

For both panfish and larger fish, anglers use a "jigging pole," which is a short stiff type rod (without a reel), designed for the up and down action of jigging. The advantage of the panfish or deep-water pole over the jigging pole is the reel; it allows you the ability to play the fish, especially larger ones while the jigging or hand line methods don't.

If you choose not to invest in either of these poles and still want to ice fish, you can use a plain hand line or your typical spinning or bait casting rod and reel. The line choice for any of the above mentioned methods can vary from 2 to 4 pound test for panfish, perch, and trout, and 8 or 12 pound test for larger fish (walleye, pike, muskie, and so forth). The following illustration shows one of the more popular setups used for the rod or hand line method of ice fishing.

GENERAL TIPS

■ Early Ice: Fish near the bottom in 10 to 20 feet of water, generally in the late afternoon.

■ Midseason: Fish deeper pockets (generally at midday) or shoals in the early morning or evening.

■ Late Season: Fish off the bottom in weedy flats, inlets, or outlets, generally at midday to dusk.

PRESENTATION

■ Try adding small pieces of cheese or marshmallow to your ice fishing lures to improve your offering when fishing for panfish.

BASIC SETUP

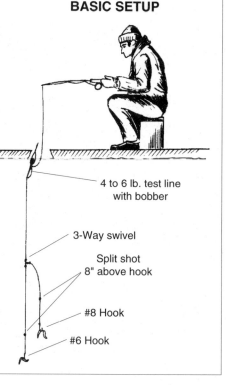

4 to 6 lb. test line with bobber

3-Way swivel

Split shot 8" above hook

#8 Hook

#6 Hook

TIP-UP TECHNIQUE

Tip-ups are devices used mostly for larger fish like the northern pike, muskie, and lake trout. They are cheap to buy and come in a variety of configurations, or they can easily be made. They are nothing more than an "X-member frame" that spans the ice hole, with a reel and line submerged under the water and a spring-type flag device that is triggered when the line is pulled or the reel moves to alert the angler when a fish bites.

The line is pulled in rapidly, hand over hand by the angler until the fish is near the hole, then it's played carefully until it's ready to be landed. The following are a few tips to try, and an example of a typical tip-up.

TYPICAL TIP-UP SETUP

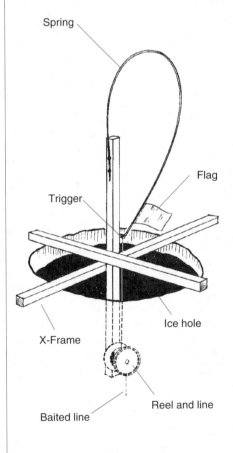

Spring

Flag

Trigger

X-Frame

Ice hole

Baited line

Reel and line

TIP-UP TIPS

■ To prevent the trigger mechanism from freezing, put a dab of Vaseline at the bottom of the trip wire that holds the spring in place.

■ When setting up tip-ups, avoid setting them all at the same depth. When you start catching fish at a specific depth, you can reset them to the proper depth. If they stop biting, go back to the "scattered" depths.

■ To keep your tip-up holes from freezing up, cut a hole in a few pieces of carpeting and place them over your holes in the ice and under the tip-ups.

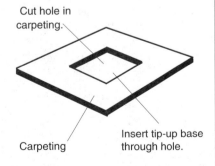

Cut hole in carpeting.

Carpeting

Insert tip-up base through hole.

The following is a quick reference chart for selecting lures or baits to use for the more commonly sought species when ice fishing. Also included are suggestions on locations and depths to try for the various species.

Species	Presentation	Location/Depths
Bluegills/Crappies	Small ice flies, teardrops, grubs, mousies, wax worms, corn, goldenrod borers, acorn borers	Weedy flats, inlets, outlets, 10-20 feet deep near bottom
Perch	Russian spoons, minnows, wigglers, teardrops, mousies, flicker spinners, french spinners, red yarn flies	Deeper pockets, shoals 6 to 24 inches off bottom
Walleye/Saugers	Leadhead jigs, Russian spoons, Swedish pimple, Rapala spoons (baited with 2-3" minnows)	Deeper pockets, shoals 15-30 feet deep, 6-8 inches above bottom
Lake Trout	Cut suckers, minnows, red or yellow flies, Swedish pimple, small spoons, spinner attractors	Deep water 50 feet or deeper 12 inches off bottom
Brown/Rainbow Trout	Corn borers, wigglers, minnows, crayfish, salmon eggs, small cheese bits, canned corn	Inlets or outlets with current, deeper water 6 feet off bottom
Northern Pike	Large minnows, 4-5" suckers, smelt, herring, 6-8" perch, large golden shiners	Drop offs, weed beds, or brush piles 3-12 feet deep 1-4 feet off bottom

COLLECTING GRUBS AND LARVAE

Whether you live in the city or the country, you can find a variety of live baits for ice fishing close to your home. To prepare for the ice fishing season, it's a good practice (and a lot easier) to collect various baits (acorn or golden rod grubs) in the late fall, at which time they can be stored until you're ready to use them when the season begins.

You can also collect various baits even during the dead of winter; however, it may be a little more difficult because of the cold or snow conditions.

City residents can collect baits in their local parks, forest preserves, or along railroad tracks, or even their own backyards. Country folks can collect in many of the same places as well as additional areas such as farms, grain storage facilities, river banks, and so forth.

The following are a few examples of the types of baits to collect and where to look for them.

GOLDENROD GRUBS

The larvae of the gall moth can be found in the stems of the goldenrod plant along weed fields, railroad tracks, or the edges of wooded areas. Look for plants that have a swelling (ball) in the stem that holds the grub. You can collect the stems and remove the grubs by cutting open the gall (ball on the stem). After you remove them, refrigerate the grubs in oatmeal or bran.

You can also refrigerate the unopened galls or freeze them; they will keep for months. Avoid galls with holes in them; birds have pecked out the larvae. The grubs make an excellent bait for crappies, bluegills, and perch.

ACORN GRUBS

If you have some oak trees near you, that's the place to collect acorn grubs. The acorn grub is the larvae of the acorn weevil, which drills a hole into the acorn and deposits its eggs inside the nut.

In the late fall, collect the acorns after they have just fallen from the tree. Look for the tiny telltail hole in the meaty part of the acorn to determine which ones to collect.

Store them in a cool place with some dirt under them, and the larvae will come out and burrow into the dirt. Remove the larvae from the dirt, and refrigerate them until you want to use them.

GRUBS AND LARVAE (continued)

WOOD BORER LARVA

Various insects (June bugs and other scarab beetles) burrow into or under rotting stumps, logs, or fallen trees for protection from the cold during the winter months.

You can find all sorts of grubs and larvae under the bark or by digging around the rotting areas. The grubs you find will be white with a darker head and about one-inch long.

WASP LARVA

The larvae of a wasp (paper or mud dauber) are excellent ice fishing baits for panfish. They are off-white in color and about 1-inch long. During the winter months, look for wasp nests in trees, brush piles, or even the eaves around your home.

Break the nests open to collect the larvae; however, when you do, make sure you do it out of doors when it's cold outside.

WAX WORMS

Wax worms are the larvae stage of the wax moth, which deposits its eggs in old honeycombs. If you know a beekeeper, ask him or her for some of their old stored brood combs. More than likely they will be more than happy to give them to you.

The larvae inside the combs will be about one-inch long and grayish-white in color. They are an excellent ice fishing bait for most species.

MEALWORMS

Mealworms are the larvae of the darkling beetle. They are about one-inch long and are yellow or brown in color. If you have a grain elevator or a feed mill near you, that's the place to go to collect them.

Sift through piles of rotting grain around the elevator, mill, or the train cars that transport the grain. Mealworms are excellent for most panfish.

LIVE BAIT SELECTION BY SPECIES

The following are the most frequently selected live baits (by species) used by ice fishermen when ice fishing.

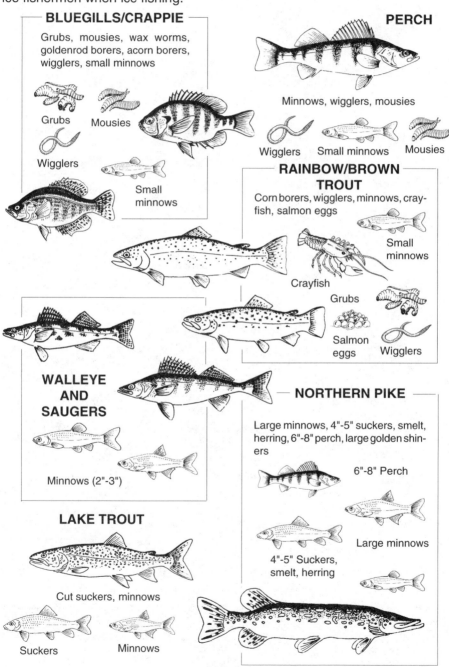

BLUEGILLS/CRAPPIE

Grubs, mousies, wax worms, goldenrod borers, acorn borers, wigglers, small minnows

Grubs

Mousies

Wigglers

Small minnows

PERCH

Minnows, wigglers, mousies

Wigglers Small minnows Mousies

RAINBOW/BROWN TROUT

Corn borers, wigglers, minnows, crayfish, salmon eggs

Small minnows

Crayfish

Grubs

Salmon eggs Wigglers

WALLEYE AND SAUGERS

Minnows (2"-3")

NORTHERN PIKE

Large minnows, 4"-5" suckers, smelt, herring, 6"-8" perch, large golden shiners

6"-8" Perch

Large minnows

4"-5" Suckers, smelt, herring

LAKE TROUT

Cut suckers, minnows

Suckers Minnows

141

LIVE BAIT FISHING

When using baits like grubs, wigglers, spikes, and so forth, avoid using split shot whenever possible.

Unweighted baits naturally drift down slowly allowing suspended fish to bite, and enable you to detect even the slightest nibble.

Unweighted baits also enable you to jig more effectively with the bait jumping up with each flick of the rod and slowly floating down again.

WARM BAIT

When you're on the ice, make it a point to keep your live bait (maggots or other live grubs) in a container in an inside pocket. Your body heat will keep them warm, making them more lively. Empty 35 mm film containers work great for holding bait.

BAIT CHECK

When using tip-ups, check your bait every 20-25 minutes. Make sure it's free of weeds and lively.

RAISING YOUR OWN

Here's a simple way to have a ready supply of mealworms and wax worms for ice fishing.

Mealworms

Put some mealworms(about 100) in a two-gallon jar 3/4 filled with a mixture of sawdust and flour, and punch a few small air holes in the lid.

The mealworm larvae will mature into darkling beetles, which lay their eggs in the mixture, generating more mealworms in a few weeks.

Wax worms

Put some wax worms (one to two dozen) in a 2-quart jar containing a mixture of 14 ounces cornflakes, brewer's yeast, and 2 ounces of grated beeswax. Combine this with a mixture of 6 ounces of glycerine, 7 ounces of honey, and 3 ounces of water. Cover the jar with mesh, and keep it in a dark place until the larvae come to the surface.

When the larvae start coming to the surface, insert a piece of pleated waxed paper in the jar. The larvae will spin their cocoons on the waxed paper and mature into adult moths within a few days. The mature moths will lay their eggs on the paper, at which time the paper should be removed from the jar, and transferred to another jar containing the same mixture. In about a week, the eggs will hatch into new larvae and grow to bait size. Keep repeating the process, and you will have a steady supply of bait for the entire fishing season.

TIPS ON LOCATING FISH

LOCATIONS

If you're familiar with the waters you're fishing, a good rule to follow to locate fish is to fish the same locations where you found fish during open water fishing. If you're not familiar with the lake or pond, you can try some of the following.

On small ponds or lakes, drill your first holes in shallow water. If nothing happens within a reasonable amount of time (1/2 hour), move and drill your next set of holes about fifteen feet farther out. Continue doing this until you reach the middle of the pond or lake or you start catching fish.

Other locations to try are inlets or creeks where they enter the pond or lake. Be careful when you try these spots; the ice can be dangerous. Also look for weed beds that form a break line to deeper water or have a drop off.

The following are a few additional useful tips for locating fish.

GETTING INFORMATION

The best place to get information about ice fishing (where, when, and how to fish) is your local bait shop or from the local people fishing the area.

Spend some time in the shop; chances are you'll meet a lot of the locals.

WEED TIP

Dead vegetation (brown) is usually void of fish. Look for weeds that have some green. If you can't find any, try the sparser areas of the brown weeds—the thicker the brown weeds, the less chance of finding fish.

Fish the edges that form break lines and have access to deep water or a drop off.

MOBILITY

One secret to catching fish through the ice is mobility.

As a rule, don't spend a lot of time in one given location. If the fish aren't biting, keep moving until you find active fish. Moving is important in making consistent catches.

ELECTRONIC LOCATORS

One of the best tools to have and to use to locate fish through the ice is a electronic locator.

Flasher type locators work the best, not only for determining the depth to fish at, but also for spotting fish and where your presentation is located.

LURE SELECTION BY SPECIES

The following are the most frequently selected lures (by species) used by ice fishermen when ice fishing.

BLUEGILLS/CRAPPIE
Ice flies, teardrops, small jigs

Ice flies

Spider

Ant

Teardrops

Small jigs

PERCH

Russian spoons, ice flies, teardrops

Russian spoons

Teardrops

Ice flies

RAINBOW/BROWN TROUT
Russian spoons, Swedish pimples, Rapala jigs, leadhead jigs, teardrops. ice flies, yarn flies

Ice flies

Teardrops

Russian spoons

Swedish pimples

Rapala jigs

WALLEYE AND SAUGERS
Russian spoons, Swedish pimple, rapala jigs, leadhead jigs

Leadhead jigs

Russian spoons

Swedish pimples

Rapala jigs

NORTHERN PIKE

Russian spoons, Swedish pimples Rapala jigs, Airplane jigs

Airplane jigs

Russian spoons

Rapala jigs

Swedish pimples

LAKE TROUT

Russian spoons, Swedish pimples, rapala jigs, airplane jigs

Russian spoons

Airplane jigs

Swedish pimples

144

EQUIPMENT TIPS

CUTTING HOLES

The key to cutting holes in ice is using a sharp tool. Regardless of the type, (spud, hand auger, or a power auger) the cutting blades or edge must be razor sharp. That's the key to making the holes quick and easy.

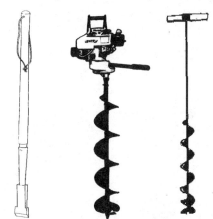

ICE SPUD TIP

Drill a hole in the handle near the top of your ice spud (if it already doesn't have one) and attach a lace strap that can be looped around your wrist to prevent loosing the spud when it goes through the ice.

ICE HOLE CLEANER

The small dip net used by tropical fish fanciers works great to remove ice chips from your ice fishing hole.

DEPTH FINDERS OR FISH LOCATORS

Using a depth finder or a fish locator for ice fishing is a priceless tool for locating and catching fish. A good quality flasher type unit works the best and can be used to identify depth, structure, fish, and bait location. As long as the ice surface is smooth and wet, you can get a depth reading directly through the ice, eliminating cutting a lot of unnecessary holes.

BAIT BUCKET

A styrofoam bucket with a lid works best for live minnows when you are ice fishing. The insulating qualities of the container will keep the water from freezing better than most other types of containers.

EMERGENCY GAFF

If you hook a lunker, and you don't have a gaff, use the curved handle of your ice spoon. Slip the handle under the gill cover and haul the fish out of the hole.

TACKLE/TECHNIQUE CHART

The following is a quick reference chart for selecting tackle and techniques to use for the more common sought species when you are ice fishing.

Species	Recommended Tackle	Techniques
Bluegills/Crappies	3-5 foot limber fiberglass rod with 4-6 lb. test line, small bobbers or spring bobbers, and no. 6-8 size hooks.	Jiggle your bait 6 to 24 inches off the bottom.
Perch	3-5 foot limber fiberglass rod with 6-8 lb. test line, small bobbers or spring bobbers, and no. 6-8 size hooks.	Fish your bait 6 to 24 inches off the bottom, using a jigging motion, or directly on the bottom.
Walleye/Saugers	Light tackle tip-ups, with 6 lb. test line and small treble hooks or hand line fishing using 6-8 lb. test line.	Allow your bait to hit bottom, then raise it a little and jig your line once every minute.
Lake Trout	Tip-ups or chugging sticks or rods with 100 yards of 10 lb. test dacron line, plus 25 feet of 15 lb. test monofilament with size 10 or 12 treble hooks or size 6-10 single hooks.	Chug your bait about 1 foot off the bottom using a slight bobbing motion.
Brown/Rainbow Trout	3-5 foot limber fiberglass rod, with a spinning or casting reel using 4-6 lb. test line, and no. 6-8 size hooks.	Bob or jig your bait at 15 second intervals keeping it within 6 feet of the bottom.
Northern Pike	Tip-ups equipped with strong monofilament line (15-20 lb. test) with a wire or gut leader weighted with a couple of no. 4 split shots, and no. 1/0 or 2/0 treble hooks.	Keep your bait between 1 to 4 feet of the bottom, checking it frequently to make sure it's lively and free of weeds.

146

LAYER SYSTEM

Most ice fishermen know that to be comfortable on the ice, you must know how to dress properly. The following "layer system," is practiced by cold weather campers, hikers, hunters, and most ice fishermen. By using the layer system, you can adapt to changing conditions and remain warm and comfortable while fishing in cold weather. Here's how it works.

ABOVE FREEZING CONDITIONS

Layer 1. Underwear: Cotton T-shirt and briefs

Layer 2. Shirt: Flannel
Trousers: Wool (loose fitting)

Layer 3. Jacket: Lightweight, windproof

BELOW FREEZING CONDITIONS

Layer 1. Underwear: Thermal-knit long johns

Layer 2. Shirt: Flannel
Trousers: Heavy down-filled

Layer 3. Coat: Down-filled with a hood

In addition to the layered body clothing, footwear should include insulated waterproof boots with one pair of light socks under a pair of medium-heavy wool socks. Head gear should consist of a wool hat with ear covers or a ski hat.

WARM HANDS

Avoid gloves that are fur or felt lined or have leather interiors. They become useless and extra cold when wet. Water resistant (both inside and out) nylon mittens work the best.

If your hands get cold, try pressing and holding them against the skin of your armpit; they will warm up quickly.

RUBBER GLOVES

Here's a tip that was passed on to me by an avid ice fisherman. To keep his hands warm, dry, and insulated against the cold, he would wear thin rubber gloves like those used in hospitals. The gloves allow flexibility when baiting, tying on, or removing hooks, and handling fish or wet lines. In addition, they could also be slipped into a pair of mittens for additional warmth.

HOMEMADE HAND HEATER

Here's a cheap way to keep your hands warm. Take along a one-pound empty coffee can with a roll of toilet paper soaked with a pint of rubbing alcohol and a small aluminum pie plate larger than the diameter of the can. When you're out on the ice, remove the plastic lid and drop in a lighted match. The blue flame in the can will quickly warm your hands and fingers. To put out the flame when you're done, cover the top of the can with the pie plate, and after it cools replace the plastic lid. Be careful with the can; it gets hot.

BAIT FISHING

Fish tend to feed less often during cold water conditions when, for the most part, they prefer smaller offerings. They are more cautious when they feed, and if your offering doesn't look right, they won't be fooled. Make sure your bait is fresh and lively. Change it as often as necessary; most baits lose their scent and wiggle after 20 minutes.

WIGGLERS

 When using wigglers, it's important to keep the lid on the container. Wigglers will deteriorate and die if exposed to light for an extended period of time.

FREEZE-DRIED BAITS

As a back-up bait, take along a few packs of freeze-dried baits such as the new larva baits, minnows, and even some dried crickets or grasshoppers. If you run out of live bait you can always use them in a pinch.

INJURED MINNOWS

Clip off part of a fin or the tail when using minnows to get more action from your offering.

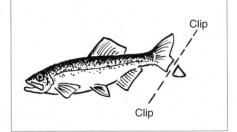

CAMOUFLAGE

When fishing on clear ice, splash some water around your hole (allowing it to freeze) to break up the clear surface of the ice. If there's snow around, scatter it around the hole. Both of these methods will make you less visible to the fish below.

DEPTH INDICATOR

When using a tip-up, returning to the same depth after you land a fish can be a problem. To solve the problem, all you need to do is to slip a small button on your line as a depth indicator. The button is adjustable and can be set anywhere on your line, which will help you to return to the same depth after a strike.

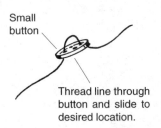

Small button

Thread line through button and slide to desired location.

ICE FISHING-SEARCH RIGS AND ATTRACTORS

Search rigs or attractors are used to attract and direct fish to the bait. They consist of a shiny object like a spinner blade or a hookless spoon rigged 2-3 inches above the bait. They can be fished in deep or shallow water using a jigging motion to get the fish's attention. The flash of the hookless lure adds the triggering power to induce the fish to bite.

SEARCH RIG

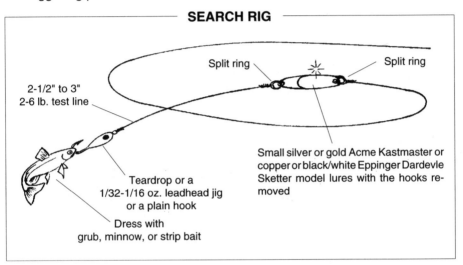

Split ring

Split ring

2-1/2" to 3"
2-6 lb. test line

Small silver or gold Acme Kastmaster or copper or black/white Eppinger Dardevle Sketter model lures with the hooks removed

Teardrop or a
1/32-1/16 oz. leadhead jig
or a plain hook

Dress with
grub, minnow, or strip bait

ATTRACTORS

A pearl button slipped onto the shank of a hook adds flash and helps fish find your bait. You can also use spinner blades in place of sinkers as an attractor.

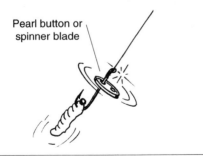

Pearl button or
spinner blade

LINE ICING

To reduce line icing, run your line through a cloth saturated with mineral oil.

MATCHES

Carry a supply of matches with you when ice fishing; you never know when you may need to build a fire to get warm, or to prevent frostbite or hypotermia if you get wet. Keep the matches in a waterproof container such as a 35mm film can.

Empty 35mm
film container

MATCHES

Matches cut
down to fit in
container

10 TIPS TO IMPROVE YOUR ICE FISHING

The following are just a few important tips to remember when you're hard water fishing.

Tip #1. If you know a good spot that produced fish during the summer, it's more than likely to produce fish in the winter. Try the productive spots you fished in the summer. Chances are the fish will be there through the ice.

Tip #2. Do your fishing with a light line. Use clear or green-colored thin diameter line, 4 to 6 lb. test.

Tip #3. Check your line frequently for line wear caused by chafing from the hole edges.

Tip #4. Make your lure or bait the center of attraction and keep it small. Use small presentations, minnows, grubs, spikes, tiny spoons, and jigs.

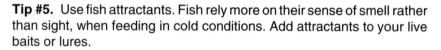

Tip #5. Use fish attractants. Fish rely more on their sense of smell rather than sight, when feeding in cold conditions. Add attractants to your live baits or lures.

Tip #6. Check your hooks. Make sure your hooks are sharp. Drag the point over your thumbnail; if it scratches the surface, it's sharp.

Tip #7. It's a good idea to fish without any sinkers in waters less than 10 feet deep.

Tip #8. When fishing without a bobber, mark your line with a marker pen to keep a consistent depth when the fish are biting.

Tip #9. Start from the bottom and work your way up slowly toward the surface to locate fish. They could be on the bottom, or suspended.

Tip #10. Don't hesitate to move if the action slows. Relocate to another hole if you can't get a bite within ten to fifteen minutes after the fish stop biting. Moving to another hole may put you back on them.

CHAPTER
8
TACKLE

Tackle Tips

Whether you fish a lot during a season or just once or twice a year, it's important to use the right equipment and to maintain it. The following pages include tips, tricks, and suggestions on selecting, purchasing, and maintaining equipment. Also included are suggestions on what type of tackle to use for specific species of fish, which should improve your ability to have a successful fishing experience.

RECOMMENDED TACKLE CHART BY SPECIES

The following chart contains general recommendations for selecting tackle for specific species of fish. The selections listed below are only suggestions to use when selecting your tackle.

RECOMMENDED TACKLE

SPECIES	ROD	REEL	LINE	LEADER
Catfish	Medium action spinning or baitcasting	Baitcasting or open or closed face spinning	6-10 lb. monofilament or braided	None
Bluegill	Ultralight spinning or 7 to 8-1/2 ft. fly	Fly or open or closed face spinning	4-7 wt. fly or 4-6 lb. monofilament	3-4 lb. fly tippet, none with spinning
Bullhead	Medium action spinning or baitcasting	Baitcasting or open or closed face spinning	6-10 lb. monofilament or braided	None
Carp	Medium to heavy action spinning or baitcasting	Baitcasting or open or closed face spinning	8-10 lb. monofilament or braided	None
Crappie	Ultralight spinning or 7 to 8-1/2 ft. fly	Fly or open or closed face spinning	4-7 wt. fly or 4-6 lb. monofilament	3-4 lb. fly tippet, none with spinning
Bass, Largemouth	Medium action spinning, baitcasting or 7-1/2 to 9 ft. fly	Fly or open or closed face spinning or baitcasting	6-8 wt. fly or 6-10 lb. monofilament or braided	6-8 lb. fly tippet, none with spinning or baitcasting
Bass, Smallmouth	Medium action spinning, baitcasting or 7-1/2 to 9 ft. fly	Fly or open or closed face spinning or baitcasting	6-8 wt. fly or 4-6 lb. monofilament or braided	6-8 lb. fly tippet, none with spinning or baitcasting
Bass, Striped	Medium to heavy action spinning or baitcasting	Open or closed face spinning or baitcasting	10-20 lb. monofilament or braided	None
Bass, White	Medium action spinning, baitcasting or 7 to 8-1/2 ft. fly	Fly or open or closed face spinning or baitcasting	6-7 wt. fly or 8-10 lb. monofilament or braided	3-4 lb. fly tippet, none with spinning or baitcasting

RECOMMENDED TACKLE

SPECIES	ROD	REEL	LINE	LEADER
Muskie	Medium to heavy action spinning or baitcasting	Baitcasting or open or closed face spinning	12–20 lb. monofilament or braided	18" Wire
Pike, Northern	Medium to heavy action spinning or baitcasting	Baitcasting or open or closed face spinning	10-15 lb. monofilament or braided	18" Wire
Sunfish	Ultralight spinning or 7 to 8-1/2 ft. fly	Fly or open or closed face spinning	4-7 wt. fly or 4-6 lb. monofilament	3-4 lb. fly tippet, none with spinning
Walleye	Light to medium action spinning or baitcasting	Baitcasting or open or closed face spinning	4-6 lb. monofilament or braided	4-6 lb.
Trout, Brown	7-9 ft. fly or medium action spinning	Fly or open or closed face spinning	4-8 wt. fly or 6-10 lb. monofilament	2-6 lb. fly tippet, none with spinning
Trout, Rainbow (Steelheads)	7-9 ft. fly or medium action spinning	Fly or open or closed face spinning	4-8 wt. fly or 6-10 lb. monofilament	2-6 lb. fly tippet, none with spinning
Salmon, Chinook	8 to 9-1/2 ft. fly or medium action spinning	Fly or open or closed face spinning	7-9 wt. fly or 10-20 lb. monofilament	10-12 lb. fly tippet, none with spinning
Salmon, Coho	8 to 9-1/2 ft. fly or medium action spinning	Fly or open or closed face spinning	7-9 wt. fly or 10-20 lb. monofilament	10-12 lb. fly tippet, none with spinning
Perch	Medium action spinning or baitcasting	Open or closed face spinning or baitcasting	4-6 lb. monofilament or braided	None

BALANCED EQUIPMENT

The following chart is a general guide for selecting the proper spinning, spincasting, or baitcasting rods and lines when using lures. Selection is based on the lure weights.

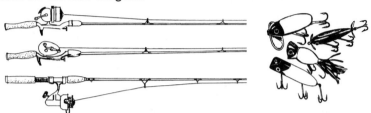

BAITCASTING/SPINCASTING OUTFITS

Lure Weight (lbs.)	Rod Length	Rod Action		Line Test
1/8 oz.	4-1/2 to 5 ft.	Ultralight	4-6 lb.	
1/4 oz.	5-1/2 to 6 ft.	Light		8-12 lb.
3/8 oz.	5-1/2 to 6 ft.	Light		8-12 lb.
1/2 oz.	5-1/2 to 6 ft.	Medium-light		8-12 lb.
5/8 oz.	6 to 6-1/2 ft.	Medium		14-20 lb.
7/8 oz.	5-1/2 to 6 ft.	Medium-heavy		14-20 lb.
1 oz. +	6-1/2 to 7 ft.	Heavy		20-30 lb.

SPINNING OUTFITS

Lure Weight	Rod Length	Rod Action	Line Test
1/16 oz.	5-1/2 to 6 ft.	Ultralight	4-6 lb.
1/4 oz.	5-1/2 to 7 ft.	Light	4-10 lb.
3/8 oz.	7 to 7-1/2 ft.	Medium-light	8-10 lb.
1/2 oz.	5-1/2 to 7-1/2 ft.	Medium-light	12-14 lb.
1/2 oz. +	7 to 8 ft.	Medium to heavy	14-20 lb.

MATCHING LURES TO EQUIPMENT
(Rule of Thumb)

Lure Type	Equipment
Plastic worms	Baitcasting, spincasting, spinning
Spinnerbaits	Baitcasting, spincasting, spinning
Jigs (1/8-1/4 oz.)	Spinning, spincasting
Jigs (3/8-1/2 oz.)	Baitcasting
Crankbaits (1/4 oz.)	Spincasting, spinning
Crankbaits (1/2-5/8 oz.)	Baitcasting
Topwater stick baits	Baitcasting
Topwater chuggers	Spincasting, spinning
Wobbler types	Baitcasting, spincasting, spinning
Minnow types (small)	Spincasting, spinning
Minnow types (large)	Baitcasting
Spoons	Baitcasting, spincasting, spinning
Buzzbaits	Baitcasting, spincasting, spinning

TACKLE BOX TIPS

The following are a few tips on purchasing, arranging, and cleaning your tackle box, as well as suggestions on additional items to add to it.

PURCHASING

Rather than buying one giant box, purchase two or three smaller boxes to use for various types of fishing. You can arrange the boxes to contain certain categories of lures, types of equipment such as spinning, casting, or salt water fishing gear, or you can set them up for "seasonal" fishing.

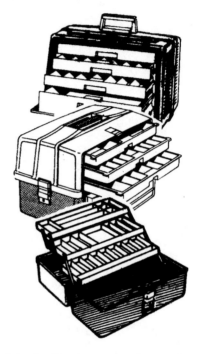

MAINTENANCE

It's a good practice to empty and clean your box and tackle after each season of fishing. To get started, wash the box with a mild detergent and some baking soda to eliminate odors. After it's dry, line the lure compartments with a cork covering.

Give your lures a close examination and polish or touch them up if they need it. Clean and sharpen the hooks on your lures and arrange them on the basis of size and color.

Clean, oil, and inspect your reels for defects. Replace, repair, or discard various items. By investing a few hours maintaining your tackle, your next season's fishing experience will be more enjoyable and successful.

TACKLE BOX EXTRAS

In addition to the general items kept in a tackle box (Lures, hooks, sinkers, swivels, and so forth), the following list of items should also be included. If not in the box, they should be readily available on any fishing trip.

- Needlenose pliers
- Small first-aid kit
- Tube or bottle of sunblock or sunscreen (summer)
- Sunglasses
- Insect repellent

- Purse-size raincoat
- Small package of Handi-Wipes
- Small pocket tool kit
- Can and bottle opener
- Small folding knife
- Small hook hone/knife sharpener
- A few Ziploc sandwich bags
- Pair of gloves (winter)
- Waterproof container of matches

PURCHASING

When purchasing a new rod, you should consider the following factors and critical features.

- Fishing method (spinning, baitcasting, fly fishing)
- Type of fish you're after
- Type of lures or bait you'll use
- Type of action, length, and power
- Material it's made of (fiberglass, graphite, or boron)

In addition, the most important feature should be how comfortable it feels in your hand.

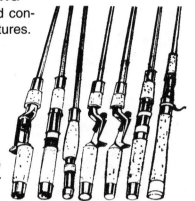

GRAPHITE ROD SELECTION

When selecting a graphite rod, four factors should be considered.

- Weight
- Strength
- Sensitivity
- Power

These factors should be applied to ultralights to magnum heavy rods.

MAINTENANCE

Before, during, and after each season, make it a point to examine your rod carefully. Check for hairline cracks in the rod blanks. Check the ferrules, line guides, and the reel seat. Clean or replace worn ferrules and line guides. Clean the hand grip with a mild detergent or with a scouring powder.

When storing your rods, never lean them against a wall or in a corner. Hang them from a rack or store them in a rigid case. With a little care, your rods will last for many seasons of enjoyable fishing.

STUBBORN FERRULES

All fishermen encounter stubborn ferrules that refuse to part. Well, here are a few tips to eliminate the problem.

For the ferrule that's really stuck, just spray a little automotive Liquid Wrench or WD-40 around the male end and let it work its way down. In a few minutes, pull the rod apart and wipe both ferrules clean.

To prevent future problems, give your ferrules a light coat of the stuff before each trip.

Another thing to do prior to assembling your rod is to rub the male ferrule in your hair, which will also give it a light oil coating. The latter tip only works if you have hair.

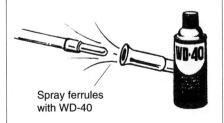

Spray ferrules with WD-40

REEL TIPS

PURCHASING

First of all, regardless of which type of reel (casting, spincast, spinning, or fly) you plan to purchase, put the reel on a rod and handle the tackle. The following are a few things to look for in the various types of reels.

Casting Reels: Good feel when palming, no thumb cramping on spool bar, easy to reach controls (antireverse, drag), easy line threading

Spincast Reels: Good feel and easy palming, easy to reach push button and controls, comfortable handles

Spinning Reels: Good feel, balance and weight, comfortable handles and stem length, easy line pick up with index finger

Fly Reels: Lightness in weight, spool capacity, interchangeable spools, smooth drag and durability

MAINTENANCE

After each fishing trip or after the season is over, it's a good practice to disassemble, clean, oil, and inspect your reels for wear. Inspect the bail arm roller guides, nose cone eyelets, and all the points where the line makes contact with the reel surface.

REEL STORAGE

It's also a good practice to loosen the drag on a reel after a day's fishing or before you put it away. Leaving the drag pressure on the spool can make the reel drag less effective.

When you're not using your reels, keep them in some kind of cloth bag or an old sock.

SETTING THE DRAG

To properly set the drag on your reel, attach the line to a fixed object such as a tree, or have a friend pull the line while you hold the rod at a 45° angle (as if you were fighting a fish).

The drag should be set at 25% of the rated breaking strength of the line by applying pressure to the line while adjusting the drag-setting knob until the line flows at a moderate line tension.

CLEANING REELS

The brush used to clean electric shavers makes an excellent tool to use when cleaning your reel. You can reach most hard-to-get spots, and in most cases, you won't have to completely dismantle the reel to clean it.

LINE TIPS

The following are a few line tips to remember to make your fishing experience more enjoyable.

LINE CAPACITY

The less line on your reel, the shorter the casting distance. Fill your reels to capacity, which in most cases is an eighth of an inch of the spool lip. If this doesn't improve the distance, switch to a lighter line; your line may be too heavy for the type of lures you are casting.

CHANGING LINE

You can save a few cents if you swap the ends of the line that is on your reel. The line on the bottom of the reel spool has never been used and will be as good as new if you reverse it on the spool. Just remember not to do it a second time.

LINE SET OR COILS

Monofilament line tends to take a set when it's reeled in wet and allowed to dry on the reel. When used in this condition during your next fishing trip, it could result in snarls, stiff coils, or tangles. To eliminate the problem, all you need to do is to soak the line in water for an hour or more before using it, which will allow the line to absorb moisture and gain limpness.

TWISTED LINE

To remove any twist or kink from your line, simply remove any hooks, snaps, or swivels from the line and troll the line behind your boat. Let out all the line on the reel before rewinding. If this doesn't work, replace your line.

THREADING LINE

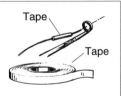

If you have ever tried to assemble your rod on a early morning or late evening fishing trip when it's pitch black out, you know how easy it is to miss a guide or lose the line during the assembly. Well, here's a perfect solution.

Before or after your trip, take the end of your line and wrap some tape around the end, forming a hard lead like a shoelace. Now, strictly by feel, you can thread the line through the guides without any difficulty. Then snip off the taped end and attach your hook or bait and you're ready to fish.

TANGLES

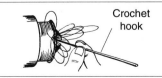

Crochet hook

A handy gadget to carry in your tackle box is a small crochet hook. It works a lot better than your fingers when picking out tangles on a reel spool.

WADERS AND HIP BOOTS

The following are a few tips on drying, repairing, and caring for your waders or hip boots.

DRYING

A mechanic's light (the type inside a cage) works great for drying boots or waders. Just slip the light into each leg and plug it into an electrical socket. In about a half hour your boots or waders will be dry.

■ ■ ■ ■

Another way to dry your boots or waders is to reverse the air flow on your vacuum cleaner. You can blow dry them in a few minutes.

■ ■ ■ ■

To prevent creases or to dry your boots or waders, you can also use the cardboard tubes that come with a roll of carpeting. For the most part, you can get the tubes at your local carpet store just by asking. Cut the tube lengths to the correct size using a hacksaw, and insert a tube in each leg. You can store your boots or waders using the tubes to prevent creases.

REPAIRING LEAKS

To find leaks, use the mechanic's light in a dark room. The light will show even the smallest leak. To repair the leak, use some clear silicone bathtub caulk. After it sets, it seals better than most other methods.

WADING SAFETY

To keep from slipping when wading, glue some old carpet scraps to the bottom soles of each foot of your waders.

WADING STAFF

The next time you're at a garage sale or a flea market and you see some old ski poles, don't pass them up.

Old ski poles make excellent wading staffs.

WADER/HIP BOOTS CARE

Never fold up a wet pair of waders or hip boots and toss them in the trunk of your car. Always hang them in a cool, shaded area with the boot part down until they dry off.

Condensation or moisture inside the waders or boots will escape more easily when they are hung with the feet down. After you get them home, try some of the above suggestions to dry them thoroughly.

HOOKS, SNAPS, SWIVELS AND SINKERS

Every fisherman has an assortment of hooks, snaps, swivels, and sinkers that at times end up loose in the lure compartments or the bottom of the tackle box, making them difficult to locate or to use. The following are a few tips on how to store them conveniently so you can find them the next time you need them.

STORING HOOKS AND SWIVELS

Instead of having loose hooks, snaps, and swivels in your tackle box, string them on either a safety pin or a paper clip. When you need them, you can find them.

Safety pin

Paper clip

PRE-TIED RIG STORAGE

Here's a neat way to store pre-tied spinner rigs, crappie rigs, walleye rigs, and snelled hooks. All you need are some Ziploc storage bags, a two- or three-ring binder, and a hole punch. Pre-tie your rigs and put them in separate storage bags. Then punch holes in either the top or bottom of the bag to fit your binder. When you plan to go fishing, just remove the bags you need from the binder and you're ready to go.

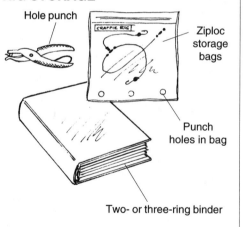
Hole punch

Ziploc storage bags

Punch holes in bag

Two- or three-ring binder

STORAGE CONTAINERS

Various items like sinkers, snaps, swivels, hooks, and so forth can also be stored in empty 35mm film containers. The containers can be labeled with a piece of tape and a marking pen and stored in a convenient location in your tackle box or carried in your pocket when you are fishing.

To obtain the containers, stop in at your local photo processing store and ask for them. Most stores will be happy to give you as many as you want.

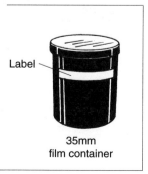
Label

35mm film container

PURCHASING LURES

What types of lures to purchase can be a problem because of the vast assortment of types, colors, and shapes available on the market. Every lure manufacture totes his products as the greatest fish catchers ever invented, and in many cases, most of them only catch the fisherman rather than fish.

To help simplify the matter of selecting and purchasing lures, the following pages are examples of the best lures to use for the most frequently fished game fish. They are proven fish producers when fished properly and should be included in your fishing arsenal.

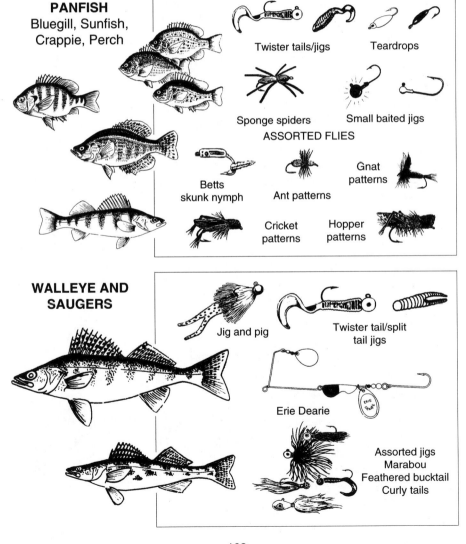

PANFISH
Bluegill, Sunfish, Crappie, Perch

Twister tails/jigs

Teardrops

Sponge spiders

Small baited jigs

ASSORTED FLIES

Betts skunk nymph

Ant patterns

Gnat patterns

Cricket patterns

Hopper patterns

WALLEYE AND SAUGERS

Jig and pig

Twister tail/split tail jigs

Erie Dearie

Assorted jigs
Marabou
Feathered bucktail
Curly tails

RECOMMENDED LURES FOR SPECIFIC SPECIES

MUSKIE

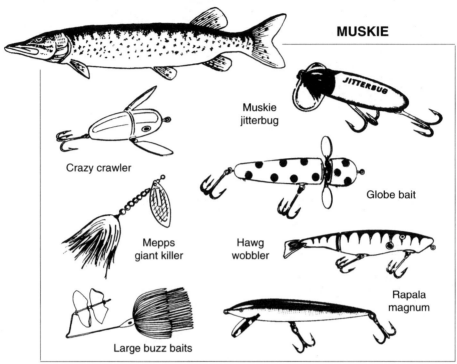

Crazy crawler

Muskie jitterbug

Globe bait

Mepps giant killer

Hawg wobbler

Rapala magnum

Large buzz baits

NORTHERN PIKE

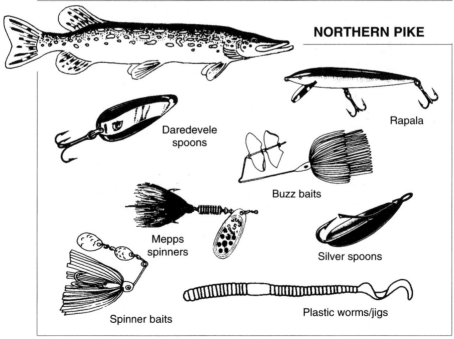

Daredevele spoons

Rapala

Buzz baits

Mepps spinners

Silver spoons

Spinner baits

Plastic worms/jigs

RECOMMENDED LURES FOR SPECIFIC SPECIES

TROUT
Steelhead, Rainbow, Brown

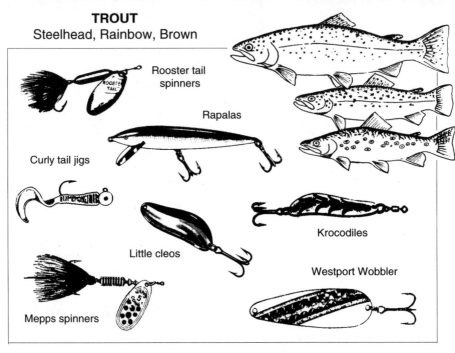

Rooster tail spinners

Rapalas

Curly tail jigs

Little cleos

Mepps spinners

Krocodiles

Westport Wobbler

SALMON
Chinook, Coho

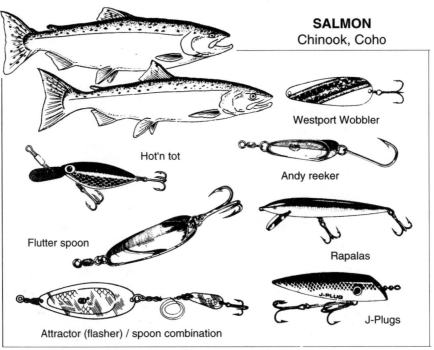

Westport Wobbler

Hot'n tot

Andy reeker

Flutter spoon

Rapalas

Attractor (flasher) / spoon combination

J-Plugs

LARGEMOUTH BASS

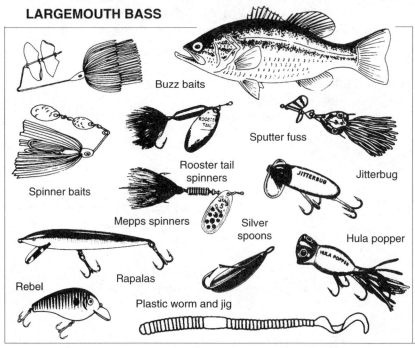

Buzz baits

Sputter fuss

Rooster tail spinners

Jitterbug

Spinner baits

Mepps spinners

Silver spoons

Hula popper

Rebel

Rapalas

Plastic worm and jig

SMALLMOUTH BASS

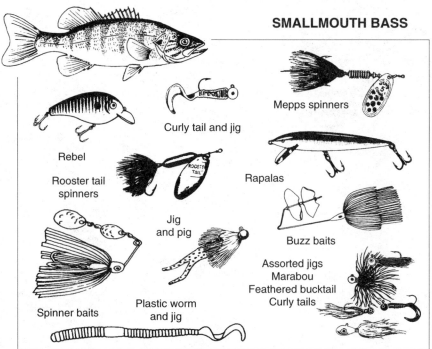

Mepps spinners

Curly tail and jig

Rebel

Rapalas

Rooster tail spinners

Jig and pig

Buzz baits

Assorted jigs
Marabou
Feathered bucktail
Curly tails

Spinner baits

Plastic worm and jig

LURE ENHANCEMENTS

The following are a few tips on how to make your lures more effective to produce better results.

SPOONS

Spoons: Wobbling spoons can be made more effective when you are fishing for bass by adding a plastic worm to the hook. The worm makes the spoon more snakelike.

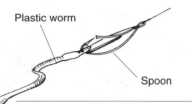

Plastic worm

Spoon

RATTLE LURE

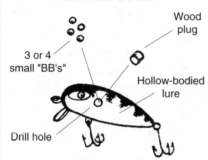

Wood plug

3 or 4 small "BB's"

Hollow-bodied lure

Drill hole

Hollow-bodied plugs: By drilling a hole the size of a BB into a hollowed-bodied plug, it can be converted into a rattle lure. All you need to do is to carefully drill a hole in the lure and insert three or four BB's inside. Then seal the hole with a small wooden plug and a dab of cement. In most cases, the BB's won't affect the action of the lure.

QUICK CHANGE SPINNERS

Spinners: Most spinners have treble hooks fastened to the body with a split ring. To make the spinner more versatile, remove the treble hook and replace it with a snap. By adding the snap, you can change to different colored buck tails, fly patterns, or plain hooks quickly and easily.

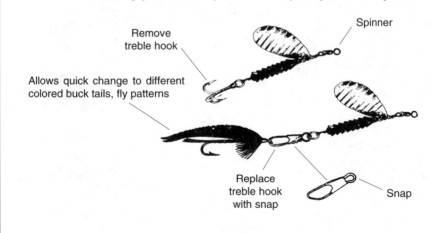

Remove treble hook

Allows quick change to different colored buck tails, fly patterns

Spinner

Replace treble hook with snap

Snap

MISCELLANEOUS EQUIPMENT TIPS

SOFT PLASTIC LURES

At one time or another, you probably have seen what happens when soft plastic lures like twister tails, grubs, or plastic worms are brought into contact with other plastics.

They melt and become one big unusable blob or mess that has to be discarded. To eliminate the problem, avoid mixing them together and store each type in their own seperate Ziploc storage bag with a little talcum powder.

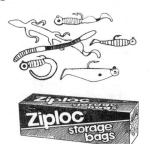

RUBBER SKIRTS

When storing spinnerbait, buzzbaits, or any lure with a rubber skirt, it's a good practice to try the following.

1. Make sure they are dry. Before you remove the lure from your gear, allow it to hang about 12 inches below your rod tip and spin the lure around in a circle 8 or 10 times. The spinning motion will fling out most of the water in the skirt.

2. After you remove your lure, sprinkle a little talcum powder on the skirt before putting it back in your tackle box.

REEL POUCHES

If you have an old flannel shirt, jacket, or pants with button-flap pockets you plan to throw away, try the following.

Cut out the button-flap pockets and use them to store your reels. They make great pouches and will accomodate most reels.

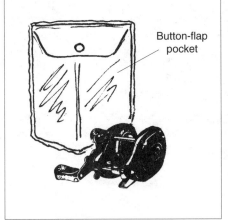

Button-flap pocket

REEL CARE

If you use a closed face spinning reel, it's a good practice to remove the spool cover after a day's fishing.

Not only will it allow the line to dry, it will also reduce the chances of corrosion and your line will last longer.

Remove spool cover

167

BAIT BUCKET TIP

To get rid of stale musty oders, fill the bucket with water and mix in a handful of baking soda. Let it stand over night and then rinse it out the next morning.

COOLER TIP

If you ever use a cooler to hold your catch and it starts to smell, clean it with baking soda.

Baking soda won't scratch the surface, and it leaves a fresh smell in the cooler until your next trip.

BUILT-IN RULER

Here's a way to always have a ruler with you that you can't misplace. All you need is some bright nail polish. Starting at the butt end of your rods or landing net, mark off one-inch increments with the nail polish.

Do the marking on all your rods and your net. That way, no matter what rod you use, you'll always have a ruler.

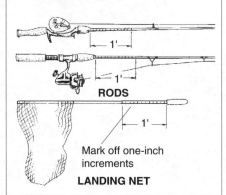

RODS

Mark off one-inch increments

LANDING NET

LANDING NET

Have you ever opened you car trunk to take out your gear and found it tangled in the landing net?

Well, to eliminate the problem, just slip a large trash bag over the net and secure it to the handle with one of the ties you get with the bags.

MAKESHIFT RAIN GEAR

In an emergency, a large plastic trash bag can be used as a raincoat. All you do is cut a hole large enough for your head in the bottom of the bag, and two holes on each side for your arms.

For headgear, use a large Ziploc storage bag after you slit open one of its sides.

SUPER FLY PATCH

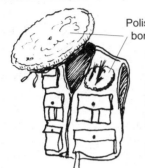

Polishing bonnet

A lamb's wool polishing bonnet used on a hand drill to polish cars makes an excellent fly patch.

It's much larger than the standard patch used on a fishing vest and will hold dozens of flies including larger streamers, bucktails, and bass poppers.

It can be sewn permently to your vest, or it can be pinned in place.

FRAYED WINDINGS

To make your rod windings look like new, wash the windings thoroughly and allow them to dry; then try some of the following methods.

Method 1. Mix up a two-part clear epoxy cement and give the windings a light coat of the mixture using a pipe cleaner. Allow the epoxy to dry for a few days until it hardens. The epoxy coating is almost indestructible and will outlast most other methods.

Method 2. Apply clear nail polish to the windings and allow it to dry.

WHAT SIZE SINKER OR JIG TO USE?
(Rule of thumb)

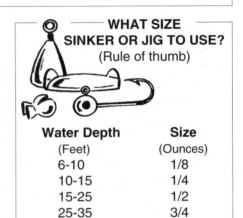

Water Depth (Feet)	Size (Ounces)
6-10	1/8
10-15	1/4
15-25	1/2
25-35	3/4
35+	1-1/2

LINE MINDER

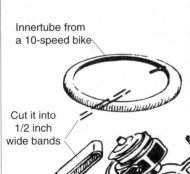

Innertube from a 10-speed bike

Cut it into 1/2 inch wide bands

Many fishermen use rubberbands to keep monofilament line from unraveling from line spools or reels.

They work great for a time, but rubberbands sometimes melt and deteriorate after a while and can get into the line windings causing a big mess.

A better way to tame your line is to get an old innertube from a 10-speed bike and cut it into 1/2-inch wide bands. The bands should be cut at a slight angle to allow you to easily pull them off your reels or line spools.

MISCELLANEOUS EQUIPMENT TIPS

DIME SCREWDRIVER

A dime makes a pretty good screwdriver in a pinch.

It's a good idea to keep one in your tackle box.

ROD TIPS

Here's a way to add a keeper ring to your rod if it doesn't have one. Cut a common paper clip or a safety pin as shown below and attach it just above the grip using rod winding thread.

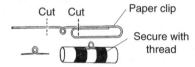

Cut   Cut   Paper clip

Secure with thread

REPELLENTS

Nothing can cause more suffering and pain or ruin a fishing trip faster than a bug attack. Whether it's mosquitoes, gnats, or deer flies, always carry a spray-can, small bottle, or a stick of insect repellent. A little dab will do it to keep the pests away.

INSTANT REFINISHING

If your old spoons or plugs have lost their shine, here's a simple trick to give them a silvery finish.

Just wrap them tightly in aluminum foil.

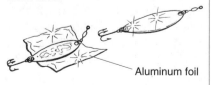

Aluminum foil

SAFETY PIN ROD REPAIRS

Emergency rod guides or a tip guide can be easily made from a common safety pin.

For rod guides, bend the two ends at right angles using a pair of pliers and snip off the safety end and the point.

Flatten the ends with a hammer (if available) so they can be firmly secured in place with thread or line or taped in position until you can make a permanent repair.

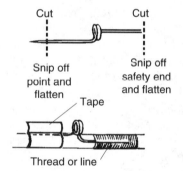

Cut   Cut

Snip off
point and   Snip off
flatten   safety end
              and flatten

Tape

Thread or line

For a temporary tip guide, bend the pin as shown below and snip off the wire at the safety end. Attach it to the rod tip with tape, thread, or line until you can get new tip guide and make a permanent repair.

Cut   Snip off
            safety end

Secure with tape,
thread or line.

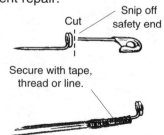

CLEANING TIPS
AND COOKING METHODS

Cleaning Tips and Cooking Methods

This chapter is devoted to what to do with the fish after you catch them. The first thing to consider is whether you plan to keep or release them.

In today's environment, with the growing interest in fishing, if we are to preserve the quality of the sport for both ourselves and future generations, we must start practicing catch and release.

We must be aware that our game fish are a great natural resource that must be conserved like anything else of value.

Rather than keeping everything you catch, you should only keep what you plan to use and release the rest. Included in this chapter are basic methods for cooking your catch, recipes, cleaning tips, and tips on how to store and care for your catch.

COOKING METHODS AT A GLANCE

The following chart is a quick reference for selecting a cooking method for a specific species of fish. The methods indicated in the chart are only recommendations, which for the most part are the most frequently used.

QUICK REFERENCE COOKING METHOD CHART

SPECIES	Broil	Bake	Grill	Pan Fry	Deep Fry	Oven Fry	Hot Smoke	Cold Smoke	Pickle
Catfish	X		X	X		X	X		
Bluegill	X	X	X	X	X	X			
Bullhead	X		X	X		X			
Carp	X	X					X		
Crappie	X	X	X	X	X	X			
Bass, Largemouth	X	X	X	X	X	X			
Bass, Smallmouth	X	X	X	X	X	X			
Bass, Striped	X	X	X	X	X	X			
Bass, White	X	X	X	X	X	X			

COOKING METHODS AT A GLANCE

QUICK REFERENCE COOKING METHOD CHART

SPECIES	Broil	Bake	Grill	Pan Fry	Deep Fry	Oven Fry	Hot Smoke	Cold Smoke	Pickle
Muskie	X	X	X	X	X	X			
Pike, Northern	X	X	X	X	X	X			X
Sunfish	X	X	X	X	X	X			
Walleye	X	X	X	X	X	X			
Trout, Brown	X	X	X	X	X	X	X	X	
Trout, Rainbow (Steelheads)	X	X	X	X	X	X	X	X	
Salmon, Chinook	X	X	X	X	X	X	X	X	
Salmon, Coho	X	X	X	X	X	X	X	X	
Perch	X	X	X	X	X	X			

COOKING METHODS

There are literally a thousand different ways to cook fish, and most are listed in the countless cook books available today. The following simple preparation methods are the basis for the majority of the recipes used in the treatment of fish. Once you've mastered the basic methods, you can master most of the recipes.

BROILING

Wipe the whole fish or the pieces with a damp cloth. Turn on the broiler and preheat a broiling pan. Remove the pan from the broiler, grease lightly, and place the fish or fish pieces in the pan.
Return the pan to the broiler at the proper distance from the heat source as follows:

2" below flame for 1/4" thick pieces
3" below flame for 3/4" thick pieces
4" below flame for 1-1/2" thick pieces
6" below flame for thicker pieces.
The general broiling time for most fish is 10 minutes for 1 inch of thickness.

BAKING

To bake fish, preheat your oven to 425°. Also preheat a large, shallow baking pan in the oven. Remove the pan and put butter and oil in the pan and swirl it until the butter melts (should be about 1/8" deep).

Wipe the whole fish or serving size pieces with a damp cloth and place them in the pan turning them over to coat both sides. Apply desired seasoning and place the pan into the oven.

Bake the fish for 10 minutes or until it flakes when prodded with a fork. The general baking time for most fish is 10 minutes per 1 inch of thickness.

BARBECUING

Start your fire about 45 minutes prior to cooking. Wipe the whole fish or pieces with a damp cloth. Season the fish as desired (inside and out) or marinate prior to cooking. Grease the grill and arrange as many pieces on the grill as will fit over the coals.

Baste the fish with butter, or a marinade of your choice. Grill the fish until it is brown and flakes readily when prodded with a fork. The general grilling time is the same as baking: 10 minutes for 1 inch of thickness.

PAN-FRYING

You can use any form of fish such as fillets, steaks, or small whole fish with this method. To fry, you will need a wide large frying pan or skillet.

Start by wiping the fish with a damp cloth, and coat the fish with the desired coating (seasoned flour, crumbs, beer batter, or tempura). Then heat butter and oil in the pan until it foams but doesn't brown (about 1/8 inch deep). A mixture of 1 part melted butter plus 2 to 4 parts of vegetable oil works fine. Place the fish, as many as will fit in the pan, into the oil, turning each piece carefully with a spatula to brown both sides.

Cook all the pieces over a low flame for about 2 or 3 minutes on each side, or until they flake readily when prodded with a fork.

DEEP-FRYING

Deep-frying can be done in a deep-fryer, large deep pan, or a wok. You can use any form of fish such as fillets, steaks, or small or large whole fish.

Start by wiping the fish with a damp cloth, and coat the fish with the desired coating (crumbs, beer batter, or tempura).

Put about 1/2 to 3/4 of an inch of cooking oil in the pan and heat until it reaches 375° (check the oil temperature with a cooking thermometer). Place the fish (one at a time) into the oil, cooking several pieces at a time until they are a golden brown. Be careful not to add too many pieces at a time; this may lower the oil temperature. Cook all the pieces about 2 or 3 minutes until they are a golden brown, or they flake readily when prodded with a fork.

OVEN-FRYING

Wipe the whole fish or the pieces with a damp cloth and coat them with the desired coating. Turn on the oven and preheat a large, shallow baking pan at 500°. Remove the pan from the oven, and put butter and oil in the pan and swirl the butter until it's melted (about 1/8 inch deep).

Place the fish or fish pieces in the pan, and return the pan to the oven. Cook the fish (uncovered) about 5 minutes on each side or until they are a golden brown and flake readily when prodded in the thickest part with a fork.

HOMEMADE SMOKING CHAMBERS

If you enjoy eating fish, one of the best ways to prepare them is to smoke them. Smoking is easy, and anyone can smoke fish by building a simple smoking chamber from various items like old refrigerators, metal trash cans, or even cardboard boxes. The following homemade smoking chambers are only a few examples of how simple they are to make and how easy they are to use.

WEBER GRILL SMOKING CHAMBER

To make this type of chamber, all you need is a new galvanized 30 gallon metal trash can with a few holes or one large hole cut in the bottom, a few holes drilled near the top for some metal rods, or a wire tray to hold the fish, and some nonresinous wood to be used as the fuel.

The following illustration shows how to construct the chamber, assemble it on the grill, and how the simple setup works.

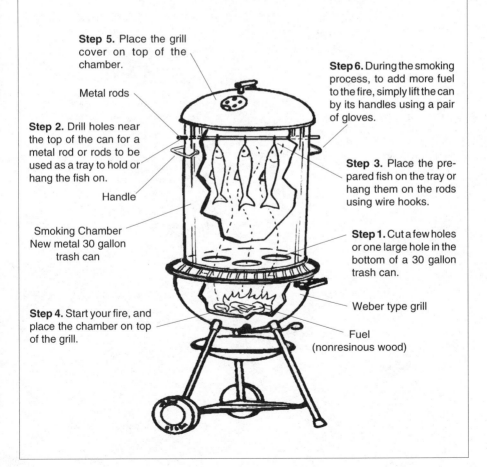

Step 5. Place the grill cover on top of the chamber.

Metal rods

Step 2. Drill holes near the top of the can for a metal rod or rods to be used as a tray to hold or hang the fish on.

Handle

Smoking Chamber New metal 30 gallon trash can

Step 4. Start your fire, and place the chamber on top of the grill.

Step 6. During the smoking process, to add more fuel to the fire, simply lift the can by its handles using a pair of gloves.

Step 3. Place the prepared fish on the tray or hang them on the rods using wire hooks.

Step 1. Cut a few holes or one large hole in the bottom of a 30 gallon trash can.

Weber type grill

Fuel (nonresinous wood)

177

30-GALLON TRASH CAN SMOKER

This type of smoker is the same as the smoking chamber used with the Weber grill. The only difference is that the trash can top will be used as the cover, and the fire source can be any type of small grill or a ground fire.

TRASH CAN SMOKING CHAMBER

Start by cutting out a large hole in the bottom (or the entire bottom) of a 30-gallon metal galvanized trash can. Next, using wire coat hangers, form a wire grill that will hang six inches below the top of the can as shown in the following illustration.

Next, cut a small hole (3" to 4" diameter) in the can cover and cover the hole with a flat piece of metal (metal plate) slightly larger than the hole in the cover. Secure the plate to the cover by drilling a small hole through both the plate and the cover and attach it using a nut and bolt. This hole will serve as the flue for the smoking chamber. The final step is to drill a hole in the cover large enough to insert a cooking thermometer stem to check the chamber temperature.

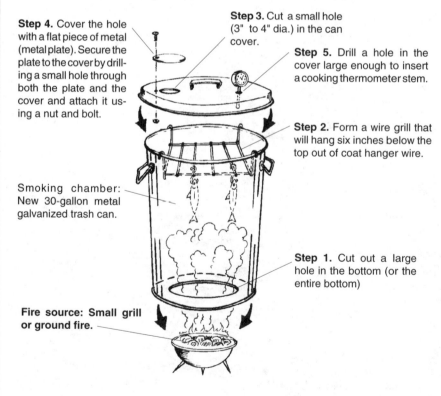

Step 4. Cover the hole with a flat piece of metal (metal plate). Secure the plate to the cover by drilling a small hole through both the plate and the cover and attach it using a nut and bolt.

Step 3. Cut a small hole (3" to 4" dia.) in the can cover.

Step 5. Drill a hole in the cover large enough to insert a cooking thermometer stem.

Step 2. Form a wire grill that will hang six inches below the top out of coat hanger wire.

Smoking chamber: New 30-gallon metal galvanized trash can.

Step 1. Cut out a large hole in the bottom (or the entire bottom)

Fire source: Small grill or ground fire.

CARDBOARD BOX (BAHAMA) SMOKER

If you want to try a really inexpensive method to smoke fish, here's how they do it in the Bahamas, using a cardboard box.

BAHAMA SMOKER

The first thing to do is to get a large firm cardboard box like a liquor carton. Open both ends of the carton and tape or tie the end flaps on one end of the carton in the open position so the box stands upright.

About six inches from the top of the other end, pierce the box with a row of metal rods or wire (coat hanger wires) to form a level grill as shown in the following illustration. Place or hook the fish you want to smoke on the wires or rod grill after you complete the standard preparation (cleaning and brining).

Next, place the carton (taped end) over a smoldering fire and close the top flaps of the box. Put a rock or a heavy object on top of the flaps to keep the flaps closed.

Smoke the fish for about four hours by adding fuel as required and watching the bottom flaps of the box so they don't catch on fire. A good preventative measure to avoid having the bottom flaps ignite is to occasionally sprinkle the lower portion of the box with water. After the smoking is completed, remove the fish and toss away the carton.

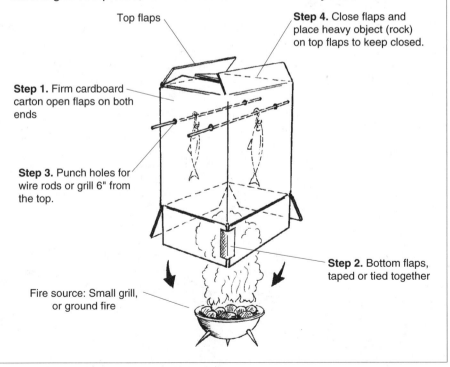

Top flaps

Step 4. Close flaps and place heavy object (rock) on top flaps to keep closed.

Step 1. Firm cardboard carton open flaps on both ends

Step 3. Punch holes for wire rods or grill 6" from the top.

Step 2. Bottom flaps, taped or tied together

Fire source: Small grill, or ground fire

SMOKING FISH

PREPARING THE FISH

Fish can be smoked whole, in chunks or fillets, depending on their size and how they will fit into the smoking chamber. The fish should be cleaned thoroughly, removing the viscera, and particularly the kidney, which is the bloody area that lies along the spine at the top of the body cavity.

With small fish, the heads could be left on, as well as the skin. With larger fish, the heads should be removed, and with some species like the pike or bass, the skin should also be removed. After they are cleaned, they can be immersed in a brine solution, salted, or marinated before smoking, which serves as a preservative and also discourages bacterial growth.

There are many different formulas for preparing fish, which are used for various smoking methods. The following are a few general formulas to try. After the fish are prepared with the various formulas, they should be rinsed off and allowed to air dry until a film (glaze) forms on the surface of the meat prior to putting them into the smoking chamber.

Brining Methods
Basic Brine: 1-1/2 cups of salt to 1 gallon of cold water. Keep the fish refrigerated in the brine solution at 40° F. for at least 12 hours.
Seasoned Brine: 4 cups of salt, 2 cups of brown sugar, 2 tablespoons of crushed black pepper, 2 tablespoons of crushed bay leaves to 1 gallon of cold water. Keep the fish refrigerated in the brine solution at 40° F. for at least 2 hours.

Salting Method
While the flesh is still wet, apply a 1/16 of an inch covering of salt over the entire fish or the fish chunks. Allow it to stand in a cool place for about an hour or until the salt has been completely absorbed by the flesh.

Marinated Method (Used for large trout and salmon)
Marinate the fish in a iced, saturated salt solution for 1-1/2 hours, then remove it from the brine and rub in a mixture of 2 pounds of salt, 1 pound of brown sugar, 1 ounce of saltpeter, 1 ounce of white pepper, 1 ounce of crushed bay leaves, 1 ounce of allspice, 1 ounce of cloves, and 1 ounce of mace. Make sure the pieces are completely covered and allow them to cure for 12 hours. Next, rinse off the mixture and allow the pieces to air dry for another 6 hours before you start the smoking process.

SMOKING PROCESS

Fuel

The best fuels to use for the smoking process are any nonresinous woods such as wood from fruit trees like the apple, plum, or cherry, which add a delicate flavor to the fish. Woods from a maple, oak, hickory, beech, alder, or birch tree are also excellent woods because they produce good smoke.

You can also use chips or sawdust from any of the above, moistened and sprinkled onto charcoal briquets to produce good smoke, and you can combine various woods and also get good results.

One thing to remember is to never use any soft woods such as pine or any other conifers, which contain pitch.

After selecting your fuel, you should start your fire at least 1 to 2 hours before you put the fish in the smoking chamber. Charcoal briquets are the best way to start the fire, and then add the moistened wood chips to produce the smoke.

Smoking Temperatures/Time

When you put the fish into the smoking chamber, the fish should be at least two to four feet away from the fire. The fire should smolder rather than burn to produce the most amount of smoke. Fish chunks or fillets should be placed skin side down toward the fire if you're using a wire rack, and should be separated so that all surfaces are exposed to the smoke.

The following chart shows the temperature and time required for the various smoking methods.

Method	Hours/Temperature
Brining Methods	
Basic	4 hours @ 120° F ., 1/2 hour @ 225° F
Seasoned	4 hours @ 225°
Salting Method	8 hours @ 180° F
Marinated Method	16-24 hours @ 100° F

MAKING LOX

Lox is a delicious form of smoked salmon with a delicate flavor which is unique to this type of smoked fish. If you haven't tried it, you're missing a real treat.

To make lox (smoked salmon), all you need to do is to modify your smoker to the cold smoking process rather than the hot smoking process generally used to smoke fish. Cold smoking is the process used to flavor fish, without actually cooking it.

Whether your smoker is a commercially manufactured one or a homemade variety, the following illustration and steps outlined below will allow you to modify your smoker to the cold smoking process. With this method, you can smoke salmon and slice it thinly enough to make lox equal to the type sold at your local delicatessen or grocery store.

COLD SMOKING PROCESS

In cold smoking, the objective is to reduce the temperature of the smoke prior to it reaching the fish. The ideal temperature to maintain when using this process is between 80 to 90°.

To accomplish this, the fish is placed in a separate chamber (wooden box) away from the heat source. The smoke is piped into the chamber via a length of stove pipe connected from the heat source to the smoking chamber. The distance between the fire source and the chamber should be a minimum of five feet; however, for cooler smoke, the distance could be greater.

The fish are smoked for about 5 hours per pound, or at least 7 hours for a whole filet. The chamber temperature of 80 to 90° should be maintained by frequent checking with a cooking thermometer. The chamber temperature should not be allowed to reach 100°.

The following illustration shows how to set up a cold smoking operation.

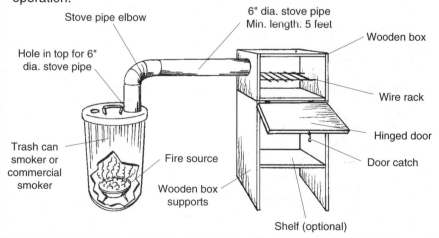

Stove pipe elbow

6" dia. stove pipe
Min. length. 5 feet

Wooden box

Hole in top for 6" dia. stove pipe

Wire rack

Trash can smoker or commercial smoker

Fire source

Hinged door

Door catch

Wooden box supports

Shelf (optional)

PICKLED FISH AND CAVIAR

HOW TO PICKLE FISH

Pickling fish is one of the easiest and oldest ways of preserving fish. When pickling, there are a few simple rules to apply to attain quality results. They are as follows:

PICKLING RULES

1. Only use fresh fish.
2. Only use soft water.
3. Use pickling salt. Don't use iodized table salt.
4. Use vinegar with a 4% acetic acid content.
5. Use fresh spices.
6. Use a glass container. Never use metal containers, metal utensils, pottery containers, or ceramic ware.
7. Refrigerate the fish during each step of the pickling process at a temperature of no higher than 40° F.
8. Consume the fish within 4 to 6 weeks.

Uncooked Fish: Start by soaking the fish in a brine solution of 1-1/2 cups of salt to 1 gallon of water for 24 hours in your refrigerator. Remove the fish from the brine solution and soak them in distilled vinegar for another 24 hours in the refrigerator.

Next, make a solution with 4 cups of vinegar, 1-1/2 cups of sugar, 8 bay leaves, and 4 teaspoons of mustard seeds, and boil it for 5 minutes and allow it to cool. Remove and drain the fish from the distilled vinegar solution, and pack them into wide-mouth jars with sliced onions between the layers of fish. Next pour the spiced vinegar over the fish and seal and refrigerate the jars for 5 days before using. The pickled fish will last up to 6 weeks.

MAKING CAVIAR

Caviar can be made from various types of fish roe. You can use sturgeon roe, which is the most common, or you can also try the roe from bluegills, northern pike, or even carp, which was originally used for caviar in China.

All you have to do is as follows.

Mix a gallon of water with enough dairy-salt to float an egg. Then add about 1/6 ounce of sodium nitrate and a pinch of sodium nitrite. Also add a teaspoon of powdered ginger and a spoon of dry or wet mustard.

Mix the solution until the salt dissolves and then place the roe into the solution after you remove it from the membrane sack.

Mix the roe in the solution for eight to ten minutes by hand, and allow it to set for an additional five minutes. Then repeat the mixing process for another five minutes or until a foam appears on the solution. Allow the roe to cure in the solution for five days at room temperature.

Remove the roe from the solution by straining it through a one-quarter or one-eighth-inch mesh and place it in jars and put it in your refrigerator until you're ready to use it. If you prefer, you can also freeze it for later use.

COOKING PANFISH

Panfish include a wide variety of smaller fish such as bluegills, sunfish, crappie, rock bass, and so forth, which provide excellent table fare when properly prepared. For the most part, as the word panfish infers, they are most often prepared by frying in a pan or skillet. However, they can also be broiled, baked or grilled and whichever method is used, their mild, tender flesh is hard to beat. The following are only a few of the traditional pan frying recipes available for preparing panfish.

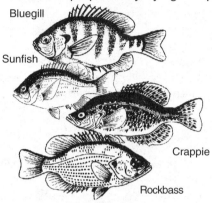

Bluegill

Sunfish

Crappie

Rockbass

FLOURED PANFISH

- 2 lbs. of panfish (fillets or whole fish)
- 2 cups of Crisco or Puritan oil
- 2 eggs
- 1/4 cup of milk
- 2 cups of flour
- Salt and pepper (as desired)

Cooking Instructions

Prepare your skillet or pan with the cooking oil. Add the desired amount of salt and pepper to the flour, mixing it thoroughly and set it aside. Next add the egg to the milk and mix both thoroughly, then dip the fish in the mixture.

Slightly drain off some of the mixture and again dip the fish into the seasoned flour. Place the fish in the heated frying pan and fry them on both sides until they get a golden brown.

Serves: 4 to 6

BEER BATTER PANFISH

- 2 lbs. of panfish fillets
- 2 cups of Crisco or Puritan oil
- 1-1/2 cups of buttermilk pancake mix
- 1 egg
- 1 teaspoon of salt
- 1-1/2 teaspoons of white pepper
- 1/2 teaspoon of thyme
- 1-1/2 cups of beer

Cooking Instructions

Prepare your skillet or frying pan by adding the Crisco or Puritan oil and heating it to 375 ° F. Next mix all the remaining ingredients together and set them aside.

Season the fillets with salt and pepper and slice them into finger size portions. Next dip the portions in the batter allowing the excess to drip off.

Place the portions in the cooking oil one at a time and fry them until they are a golden brown. Drain the portions on a paper towel and serve them with a lemon wedge.

Serves: 4 to 6

COOKING SALMON

If you're fortunate enough to live in an area where you can catch salmon or if you travel to fish for them in various parts of the country, they provide great sport as well as excellent table fare.

The following are just a few simple ways to prepare salmon, even if you purchase them at your local fish market.

Chinook

Coho

■■■■
BROILED SALMON

- 4 to 6 1" thick salmon steaks
- tablespoon of brown spicy mustard
- tablespoon of olive oil
- 1/2 cup of dry red or white wine
- 1 clove of garlic (crushed)
- Salt and pepper as desired

Cooking Instructions

Wash and pat dry the salmon steaks and place them in a well-greased broiling pan.

Next, blend together all the ingredients and lightly brush the steaks (both sides) with the sauce.

Broil about 3 inches from the heat source for 4 to 6 minutes on each side.

Serves: 6

■■■■
BAKED SALMON STEAKS

- 4 to 6 1" thick salmon steaks
- 1/3 cup melted butter
- teaspoon of Worchestershire sauce
- tablespoon of grated onion
- 1/4 teaspoon of paprika
- Salt and pepper as desired

Cooking Instructions

Preheat your oven to 350° F. Wash and pat dry the salmon steaks and place them in a shallow baking pan. Next, blend together the butter, Worchestershire sauce, onion, and paprika and lightly brush the steaks (both sides) with the mixture. Sprinkle with salt and pepper as desired and bake for 25 to 30 minutes.

Serves: 4

COOKING PERCH

Perch can be pan fried, deep fried, broiled, grilled, or baked, depending on your preference. The following are just a few of the many perch recipes to try to enjoy this wonderful tasting fish.

Perch

■ ■ ■ ■
PERCH ORIENTAL

■ 1 lb. of boneless perch fillets
■ 1 cup of broccoli
  (coarsely chopped)
■ 1 cup of pea pods
■ 1 medium size onion
  (coarsely chopped)
■ 1 medium size green pepper
  (coarsely chopped)
■ 1/4 cup chicken stock

Cooking Instructions

Using a wok or skillet, add 3 table-spoons of cooking oil and preheat the oil until it's hot. Cut the perch into small chunks about 1-1/2 inches long and fry them until they begin to flake, stirring constantly.

Remove the pieces from the oil and set them aside. Next, add the vegetables to the oil and stir-fry them over a high heat until they are firm and still crisp. Add the cooked perch pieces, the chicken stock, and salt and pepper as desired to the veg-etables and continue to stir all the ingredients gently until they are all thoroughly heated. Serve over a bed of rice with soy sauce.
Serves: 4

■ ■ ■ ■
PAN FRIED PERCH

■ 1 to 2 lbs. of perch fillets
■ 1 cup of Crisco oil or bacon
  grease
■ 2 cups of cornmeal, cracker
  crumbs, or egg batter

Cooking Instructions

Heat the oil or grease in a skillet or frying pan. Rinse and drain the fillets in cold water and roll them in the cornmeal, cracker crumbs, or egg batter.

Place the fillets in the pan or skillet and cook them until they are a golden brown on both sides.
Serves: 4 to 6

■ ■ ■ ■
PERCH CASSEROLE

■ 2 lbs. of boneless perch fillets
■ 4 pieces of lean bacon
■ 1 sliced large onion
■ 2 thinly sliced large tomatoes
■ 1/2 teaspoon of lemon juice
■ 1 can (11 oz.) cheddar cheese
  soup or cheese sauce
■ Salt and pepper as desired

Cooking Instructions

Preheat your oven to 350° F., then in a well-greased casserole, arrange the ingredients in layers in the fol-lowing order: bacon, onions, toma-toes, and seasoned perch fillets (salt, pepper, and lemon juice).

Next, spread the cheese soup or sauce over the fillets and bake in the oven for 20 minutes or until the fish flakes when tested with a fork.
Serves: 4 to 6

COOKING WALLEYE AND SAUGERS

Walleye and saugers are considered by many fishermen to be the best tasting fish you can catch. Although the walleye is considered number one, the sauger comes in as a close second when it comes to taste. When cooked properly, the tender flaky flesh is a delight to anyone's palate. The following are just a few of the great number of recipes to try to enjoy these wonderful tasting fish.

Walleye

Sauger

■■■■
PAN FRIED
WALLEYE OR SAUGER

- 1 to 2 lbs. of walleye or sauger fillets
- Crisco oil or bacon grease
- 1 egg (beaten)
- 2 tablespoons of milk
- 1 teaspoon of salt
- 1/2 cup of cornmeal
- 1/2 cup of flour

Cooking Instructions

Heat the oil or grease in a skillet or frying pan. Rinse and drain the fillets in cold water.

Combine the egg, milk, and salt in a bowl, and also combine the cornmeal and flour in a separate bowl. Dip the fish into the egg mixture and then roll them in the cornmeal-flour mixture.

Place the fillets in the pan or skillet and cook them for five minutes on each side or until they flake easily when tested with a fork.

Serves: 4 to 6

■■■■
BAKED WALLEYE
OR SAUGER

- 1-2 lbs. of dressed walleye or sauger
- 1 cup of chopped green onions
- Butter
- 1 cup of white wine
- Salt and pepper

Cooking Instructions

Preheat your oven to 425° F. Clean and wash the fish and pat dry. Using a baking pan, oil the pan and cover the bottom with the chopped green onions.

Next place the fish on top of the onions, dot it with a couple of butter pads, and sprinkle it with salt and pepper.

Add the wine to cover the bottom of the pan and bake at 425° until it flakes easily with a fork. Baste the fish during the cooking process and add additional wine and butter as needed.

Serves: 4

COOKING NORTHERN PIKE OR MUSKIE

Both the northern pike and the muskie can be memorable delights when properly prepared. Both fish have a firm, white, sweet flesh that can be baked, broiled, fried, pickled, or smoked. Both fish are usually filleted and skinned, but can also be prepared whole or in serving size portions. The following are a few simple ways to prepare both northerns and muskie.

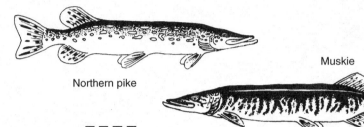

Muskie

Northern pike

■■■■
GRILLED PIKE OR MUSKIE

- 2 lbs. of boneless pike or muskie fillets
- 1/2 cup of melted fat or oil
- 1/4 cup of lemon juice
- 2 teaspoons of salt
- 1/2 tablespoon of Worcestershire sauce
- 1/4 teaspoon of white pepper
- Paprika

Cooking Instructions

Start your grill about a half hour before you cook the fish and adjust the rack to about 4 inches above the coals. Wash and cut the fish into serving size portions and combine the ingredients, with the exception of the paprika, to make the sauce.

Baste the fish with the sauce and sprinkle the portions with the paprika. Place the portions on the grill and cook them for about 8 minutes on each side while basting with the sauce (sprinkle with additional paprika if desired). Cook the fish until the flesh flakes when tested with a fork.

Serves: 4 to 6

■■■■
PICKLED PIKE OR MUSKIE

- Northern pike or muskie (cleaned)
- 1 cup of vinegar
- 1 cup of water
- 1-1/2 tablespoons of sugar
- 1 teaspoon of salt
- 1 tablespoon of mixed spices
- 1 large chopped onion

Cooking Instructions

Clean, wash, and cut the fish into small chunks that will fit into the jars you plan to use. Combine the above ingredients (with the exception of the onions) in a sauce pan and boil them for a few minutes.

Add the fish portions and continue boiling until you can pierce the fish easily with a fork. Remove the fish from the heat source and allow them to cool.

Pack the fish in wide mouth jars or an open stone jar with the chopped onions and refrigerate them for a day or two before eating.

Serves: 4 to 6

COOKING LARGE AND SMALLMOUTH BASS

Most bass fishermen, whether they fish for smallmouths or largemouths, practice catch and release these days. However, occasionally a bass dinner can be a special treat when properly prepared. Both species can be baked, broiled, grilled, or fried with excellent results. The following are just a few recipes to try if you decide to keep a few bass for the dinner table.

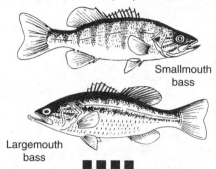

Smallmouth bass

Largemouth bass

BAKED STUFFED BASS

- 3 to 5 lbs. of cleaned and scaled whole bass
- 3 tablespoons of butter or margarine
- 1/2 cup of finely chopped celery
- 1 onion (small and finely chopped)
- 1/2 cup of sliced mushrooms
- 1/2 cup of rice
- 2 tablespoons of lemon juice
- 1/2 teaspoon of dill
- 1/8 teaspoon of thyme
- Salt and pepper as desired

Cooking Instructions

In a skillet or frying pan, cook the celery, onions, and mushrooms in the butter or margarine for six or seven minutes. Also cook the rice in a separate pot, according to the directions on the package. Drain the rice, if necessary, and combine the fried vegetables with the rice, adding the lemon juice, dill and thyme. Add seasoning (salt and pepper) as desired. Next, prepare a baking dish or pan by covering the bottom with aluminum foil and buttering it. Stuff the fish with the rice mixture and close the cavity with skewers and string.

Place the fish on the foil, cover it with a lid or more foil, and place it into a preheated 350° oven. Bake it for 50 to 60 minutes or until it flakes easily when prodded with a fork. Serves: 4 to 6

BROILED BASS

- 1 to 2 lbs. of bass fillets
- 4 tablespoons of mayonnaise
- 1 teaspoon of mustard
- 2 teaspoons of lemon juice
- 1 tablespoon of grated Parmesan cheese
- 1 tablespoon of bread crumbs

Cooking Instructions

Rinse and drain the fillets in cold water and pat them dry. Combine the mustard, mayonnaise, and lemon juice and spread it over the fish fillets. Place the fillets on a buttered broiling pan and sprinkle them with the cheese and bread crumbs. Broil 4 inches from the heat source for 6 to 10 minutes or until the flesh flakes when prodded with a fork.
Serves: 4

COOKING TROUT

If you were fortunate enough to have caught some nice trout during the season, you will certainly want to enjoy a delicious meal after you bring them home.

Trout can be prepare by broiling, baking, frying, smoking, or barbecuing and if cooked properly will provide a wonderful tasty meal. The following recipes are only a few of the many ways to prepare trout.

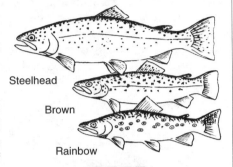

Steelhead

Brown

Rainbow

■ ■ ■ ■
BROILED TROUT

- ■ 2-1/2 lbs. of trout fillets
- ■ 3/4 cup of water
- ■ 1/4 cup of melted butter
- ■ 1/2 cup of chopped mushroom stems and pieces
- ■ 1 teaspoon of salt
- ■ Pepper as desired
- ■ 1-1/4 cup of shredded cheddar cheese
- ■ 1 teaspoon of lemon juice

Cooking Instructions

Preheat your broiler and grease your broiling pan. Place the fish in a skillet with the water and simmer for 6 minutes.

Next, in a bowl combine together the butter, salt, pepper, and lemon juice and brush the fillets with the mixture. Place the fillets in the broiling pan and cover them with the cheese and mushrooms.

Broil the fillets for 3 to 4 minutes or until the cheese is melted and bubbly.

Serves: 4

■ ■ ■ ■
BARBECUED TROUT

- ■ 1 large trout
- ■ 1/4 lemon wedge
- ■ 1/2 cup of soy sauce
- ■ 1/2 cup of cooking sherry
- ■ 1 clove of crushed garlic
- ■ 1 tablespoon of lime or lemon juice
- ■ 1/4 cup of vegetable oil

Cooking Instructions

Start your grill about a half hour before you plan to grill the fish. Next, prepare the marinade by combining the soy sauce, sherry, lemon or lime juice, vegetable oil, and garlic in a shaker and shake well. Place the fish in the marinade and let it stand for an hour turning it once.

Remove the fish from the marinade and brush the cavity with the juice from the lemon wedge and sprinkle it with herbs of your choice.

Cook the fish over hot coals on a well-greased grill basting with the marinade and turning it over once.

Cook each side for 5 to 8 minutes or until the fish flakes easily when tested with a fork.

Serves: 2

COOKING CATFISH OR BULLHEADS

Throughout many areas of the United States, as well as other locations in the world, catfish and bullheads are considered one of the best tasting fish available today. Catfish and bullheads have an exceptional delicate flavor and pleasant texture, which makes a delicious enjoyable meal when cooked properly.

They can be baked, broiled, barbecued, fried, or even smoked. Whichever method you choose, catfish and bullheads make a great meal.

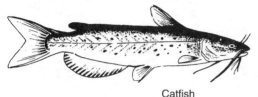

Catfish

Bullhead

■ ■ ■ ■
BAKED
CATFISH OR BULLHEADS
Southern Style

- 6 skinned, pan-dressed catfish or bullheads
- 1/2 cup of French dressing
- 12 lemon slices
- Paprika

Cooking Instructions

Preheat your oven to 350° F., and prepare a well-greased, shallow baking pan or dish. Clean, wash, and dry the fish and brush both the inside and outside with the French dressing.

Next, cut 6 of the lemon slices in half and put 2 halves in each body cavity. Place the fish in the pan, and put the remaining 6 lemon slices on top of each fish and brush the tops with the remaining dressing. Sprinkle each fish with paprika and bake them for 25 to 30 minutes or until they flake easily when prodded with a fork.

Serves: 6

■ ■ ■ ■
PAN FRIED
CATFISH OR BULLHEADS

- 6 skinned, pan-dressed catfish or bullheads
- 2 tablespoons of milk
- 2 teaspoons of salt
- 1/4 teaspoon of pepper
- 2 eggs
- 2 cups of cornmeal

Cooking Instructions

Rinse and drain the fish in cold water and pat them dry. Sprinkle both sides with salt and pepper. Next, combine the milk with the eggs by beating the eggs slightly and blending in the milk. Dip the fish in the egg batter and then roll them in the cornmeal.

Place the fish in a large frying pan or skillet containing about 1/8 of an inch of melted fat and fry at a moderate heat until one side is brown. Then turn the fish over carefully and brown the other side. Cooking time is about 10 minutes depending on the thickness of the fish.

Serves: 6

COOKING STRIPED, WHITE, AND YELLOW BASS

The striped bass family consists of the smaller white and yellow bass (often called "stripers") frequently caught in many lakes and streams throughout the United States, and the large hybrid cousin of the saltwater "striped bass" species found in many inland reservoirs and impoundments. All three types are excellent tasting fish when prepared properly. They can be broiled, baked, fried, or grilled. The following are a few recipes on how to prepare striped bass.

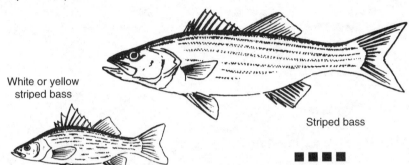

White or yellow striped bass

Striped bass

■ ■ ■ ■
BROILED STRIPED BASS

- ■ 4 striped bass steaks
- ■ 1/4 cup of melted margarine or butter
- ■ 2 tablespoons of lemon or lime juice
- ■ Salt and pepper as desired

Cooking Instructions

Preheat your broiler and prepare a broiling pan by covering the bottom with aluminum foil and buttering it. Add seasoning (salt and pepper) to the steaks as desired. Next combine the melted margarine or butter with the lemon or lime juice and baste the fish on both sides. Place the steaks four inches below the broiler flame and broil five to eight minutes per side.
Serves: 4

■ ■ ■ ■
BROILED
WHITE OR YELLOW BASS

- ■ 1 to 2 lbs. of white or yellow bass fillets
- ■ 4 tablespoons of mayonnaise
- ■ 1 teaspoon of mustard
- ■ 2 teaspoons of lemon juice
- ■ 1 tablespoon of grated Parmesan cheese
- ■ 1 tablespoon of bread crumbs

Cooking Instructions

Rinse and drain the fillets in cold water and pat them dry. Combine the mustard, mayonnaise, and lemon juice and spread it over the fish fillets.

Place the fillets on a buttered broiling pan and sprinkle them with the cheese and bread crumbs. Broil 4 inches from the heat source for 6 to 10 minutes or until the flesh flakes when prodded with a fork.
Serves: 4

CLEANING TIPS

CLEANING SHORTCUTS

SPEED CLEANING

You can do a faster and better job of cleaning fish by using two knives. Use a stiff-bladed knife for dressing and filleting, and a flexible-bladed knife for stripping off the skin.

CLEANING SMALL FISH

Use an old newspaper when you clean small fish. After each fish, just turn the page for a fresh cleaning surface. When you're finished, just bundle up the mess and throw it away.

CLEANING A LOT OF FISH

When you have an exceptional catch, and a lot of fish to fillet, try this. Wipe them dry with a cloth, and rub some salt on your hands. They won't be so slippery and will be a lot easier to clean.

SCALING FISH

To keep down the mess when scaling fish, fill a tub with water and try scaling them under the water. After you're done, just dump the mess.

SMELLY HANDS

After cleaning fish, to eliminate the odor from your hands, use a few drops of oil of anise. Another method is to wash your hands, and then lather them up again but don't rinse off the lather. Just dry your hands and the soap lather will leave them smelling fresh.

HOMEMADE CLEANING BOARD

Another way to prevent your fish from sliding around during cleaning or filleting is to make a simple cleaning board. All you need is the toe part of an old rubber boot and a board.

Instructions

Cut the toe part off the boot and secure it to the board with some nails or screws (wash the toe part first).

When cleaning the fish, place the head into the toe opening to keep the fish in place while you scale or fillet it.

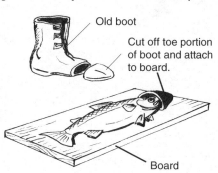

Old boot

Cut off toe portion of boot and attach to board.

Board

CATCH CARE

NO ICE

If you don't have any ice, or if it may take some time to get some, try this.

Several thicknesses of wet news-paper will make a good insulator against the heat until you can get some ice.

KEEPING FISH COOL

Here's a neat tip to keep your catch fresh. Fill some empty gallon or quart plastic milk bottles with water and freeze them a day or two before your next fishing trip. You can put them in a cooler to keep your lunch and beverages cold while you are fishing, and after you're done, you can use them to keep your catch fresh.

If the fish don't fit in the cooler, you can put them in a large plastic trash bag along with the bottles, and not worry about having a wet mess when you get home, because the melting water stays in the bottle.

STORING FISH

MILK CARTON STORAGE

Save your empty milk cartons (pints, quarts, or half-gallon sizes). After you clean your catch, just open the top of the carton at the seam, put in your fillets and fill it with water.

Fold over the top and seal it with freezer tape, then mark what's in it with a marker pen. You can stack the cartons neatly in your freezer, and when you use them, your fillets will be as fresh as when you caught them.

ZIPLOC BAG STORAGE

After you clean your catch, place it in a Ziploc plastic type bag and fill it with water and freeze it.

Not only will it retain the flavor of the fish, it will also prevent freezer burn.

CHAPTER
10
FISHING TIPS AND FISH FACTS

Fish Tips and Facts

Most successful anglers know that the more you know about fish, the easier they are to catch. With that in mind, this chapter is devoted to some basic facts regarding specific species and tips on how to pursue them.

Included are tips and recommendations on how to find them, when to fish for them, and what to use. By knowing the habits, food choices, spawning cycles, and so forth of your quarry, you will have an advantage and the ability to be more successful.

FISH FACT CHART

The following chart contains general information about specific species of fish. The information given here will vary according to climate, environment, and individual fish.

QUICK REFERENCE FACT CHART

SPECIES	AVERAGE SIZE	AVERAGE LIFE SPAN	SPAWNING PERIOD	PRINCIPLE FOOD	PREFERRED HABITAT
Catfish	2-5 lbs.	8-15 Years	Spring	Fish Insects Molluscs	Rivers
Bluegill	1/4 lb.	5-6 Years	May thru August	Insects	Lakes and ponds
Bullhead	1/2-1 lb.	4 Years	Spring	Fish Insects Molluscs	Rivers, ponds, and creeks
Carp	2-5 lbs.	7-8 Years	Spring	Insect larvae	All waters
Crappie	8 Inches	4-5 Years	Spring	Insects Fish	Lakes and streams
Bass, Largemouth	3/4 lb.	5-6 Years	Spring	Fish Crayfish	Lakes, ponds, and sluggish rivers
Bass, Smallmouth	1/2 lb.	5-6 Years	Spring	Fish Crayfish Insects	Lakes and swift rivers
Bass, Striped	15 lbs.	7 Years	Spring	Fish	Large lakes
Bass, White	1/2 lb.	3-5 Years	Spring	Fish Insects	Rivers and lakes

FISH FACT CHART

QUICK REFERENCE FACT CHART

SPECIES	AVERAGE SIZE	AVERAGE LIFE SPAN	SPAWNING PERIOD	PRINCIPLE FOOD	PREFERED HABITAT
Muskie	30 Inches	15 Years	Spring	Fish	Cold lakes and rivers
Pike, Northern	2 lb.	8-10 Years	Spring	Fish	Lakes and rivers
Sunfish	3-6 Inches	4-6 Years	May thru August	Insects	Lakes and ponds
Walleye	1-4 lbs.	10-12 Years	Spring	Fish and insects	Rivers and lakes
Trout, Brown	1 lb.	6 Years	October thru December	Insects Fish	Lakes and cold clear streams
Trout, Rainbow (Steelheads)	1 lb.	6 Years	February thru April	Fish Insects	Lakes and cold clear streams
Salmon, Chinook	18 lbs.	4-5 Years	Fall	Fish Insects	Lakes and cold clear streams
Salmon, Coho	5 lbs.	3-4 Years	Fall	Fish Insects	Lakes and cold clear streams
Perch	1/4 lb.	7-8 Years	Spring	Fish Insects	Rivers and lakes

GROWTH RATE FOR FRESHWATER FISH

The following table will give you the average age of a fish, based on its length in inches. It is only a rule of thumb, and sizes can vary depending on locations, conditions, and food supply.

SPECIES	AGE IN YEARS									
	1	2	3	4	5	6	7	8	9	10
Largemouth bass	6.3	9.0	11.6	13.5	15.8	17.4	18.9	19.8	20.3	20.7
Smallmouth bass	5.6	8.2	10.6	12.7	14.5	16.3				
Northern pike	19.0	23.5	25.2	27.8	28.4	31.1	32.5			
Muskie	7.9	15.2	21.0	26.2	30.3	33.5	37.2	41.2		
Walleye	10.1	13.2	15.5	17.6	19.3	22.1	24.6			
Yellow perch	4.1	5.8	7.7	8.6	10.0	11.0	14.3			
White bass	6.8	9.5	11.3	13.0	15.1	16.5				
Yellow bass	5.3	6.4	7.3	8.0	10.1	10.5	12.9			
Bluegill	3.2	4.6	5.7	6.6	7.4	8.4				
Warmouth bass	2.9	4.6	5.7	6.7	7.6	8.8				
Rock bass	4.0	4.5	6.6	7.7	9.0	10.0				
Pumpkinseed sunfish	3.5	4.4	5.3	5.6	6.4					
Redear sunfish	5.2	6.2	7.1	7.8	9.2	9.3	9.5			
Green sunfish	3.4	4.3	5.4	6.3	7.3	8.8				
Black crappie	6.2	7.2	7.9	10.2	10.3	10.4				
White crappie	5.3	7.2	8.3	10.6	12.2					
Bullhead	2.7	5.2	6.0	6.7	7.2	8.0	8.5	9.7	10.4	
Channel catfish	6.4	9.6	12.6	14.3	16.7	18.5	21.0	22.6	25.6	26.6
Carp	7.8	12.9	14.1	15.0	16.0	17.3	21.3	26.0	32.2	35.3
Rainbow trout	3.9	7.8	13.3	17.1	20.7	24.0	29.9			
Brook trout	3.7	5.8	7.2	12.9						
Lake trout	5.0	8.0	10.7	14.1	16.5	19.2	22.3	24.9	26.9	28.3
Brown trout	4.2	8.0	11.1	14.0	17.6	21.0	22.0			
Chinook salmon	6.0	12.0	20.0	28.0						
Coho salmon	10.0	18.0	22.0							

GROWTH FACTORS
How fast a fish grows depends on the following factors:

■ **Food Supply:** The abundance of food available.

■ **Living Space:** Fish will not grow well in overcrowded conditions.

■ **Water Conditions:** Polluted waters affect the food chain, reducing the food supply.

■ **Length of Growing Season:** Fish are most active and feed the most during the warmer months.

FISH SENSES

The following chart shows the general range of the senses (sight, hearing, smell, and vibration impulses) for most common game fish. The distance shown can vary by species.

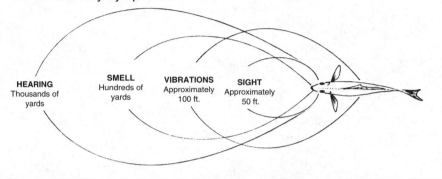

HEARING
Thousands of yards

SMELL
Hundreds of yards

VIBRATIONS
Approximately 100 ft.

SIGHT
Approximately 50 ft.

FISH EYES

The shape of a fish's eye lens is almost a perfect sphere, which is different than the somewhat flattened lens of land animals. They have excellent vision which is remarkably adapted for underwater vision. Because of the lens shape, fish are extremely nearsighted, which explains why you need to have all that accuracy when casting.

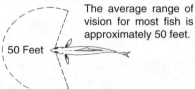

The average range of vision for most fish is approximately 50 feet.

50 Feet

Predators like the bass, pike, walleye, and trout have eyes located to the front of the head, which increases their depth perception, while other fish like the minnows, crappies, and so forth have eyes located more to the side, which increases their total field of vision.

WHAT FISH SEE
Colors, Shades, and Forms

Scientists have proven that fish can recognize certain colors and certain shades of color and relate to specific shapes and forms. Fish can distinguish the difference between red, green, yellow, and blue. These colors change or are altered as to what a fish will see as the water conditions change. The color intensity changes as the waters get cloudy or turbid. They also change at deeper depths.

Water absorbs light rapidly, the deeper the water the less color. At 25 feet, water will filter out most of the light rays that are necessary to distinguish colors. Most everything seen by a fish at that depth will appear to be black.

Even at greater depths, fish relate to shapes and forms that resemble shapes they are accustomed to seeing. Most shapes or forms that fish are accustomed to represent some form or shape in their food chain.

FISH SENSES

WHAT FISH HEAR

Fish have an inner ear which is located inside of their heads. It has no outside openings like the human ears, and it is not connected to an eardrum. However, it is located in approximately the same location as the human ear, and in some species, it is connected to the swim bladder, which acts as a sound amplifier. Sounds are transmitted through the water through the skin and bones of the fish's head directly to the ear. It is normally used for long-range hearing, and this hearing apparatus is so sensitive, it can detect sounds or vibrations thousands of yards away.

Inner ear

LATERAL SENSE LINES

In addition to the inner ear, fish also have a very sensitive series of minute organs known as the "lateral sense line" along each side of their body. This sense line is used for close range sounds or pressure waves created in the water up to 100 feet away. Any sounds that are transmitted through the airwaves (above the water or ground) can't be detected by a fish. However, sounds (vibrations) caused by walking near the water, or in a boat on the water, will transmit vibrations into the water, which can be detected by a fish.

Lateral sense line

WHAT FISH SMELL

Fish have a highly developed olfactory sense which is a large part of their brain. The olfactory openings (nostrils) are located above the mouth on the forward part of the head.

Scientists have proven that fish use this highly developed sense of smell and taste when feeding.

Certain species of fish rely on their sense of smell more than others.

Scavengers such as catfish, bullheads, carp, and even lake trout use their nostrils to locate food, while most predators such as pike, muskie, and bass are more sight orientated rather than depending on smell when searching for food. Most fish can detect odors hundreds of yards away or as minute as one part in 80,000,000 parts of water.

Many foreign odors such as human scent, oils, gasoline, or nicotine drive fish away. That's why it's important to use a good scent or fish soap that conceals human or petroleum odors when you are fishing.

Nostrils

FISHING RECOMMENDATIONS

The following is a quick reference chart containing general information as to when, where, and how to fish for a specific species. Included are the more common fish species sought by most anglers.

QUICK REFERENCE FISHING CHART

SPECIES	TIME OF YEAR	SUGGESTED WATERS	SUGGESTED LOCATIONS	SUGGESTED BAITS
Catfish	July thru Sept.	Rivers and impoundments	Brush piles, riffles, deep pools, below dams	Crayfish, shrimp, large shad, stinkbaits
Bluegill	Spring, May thru Sept.	Lakes and ponds	Weed beds, stumps, brush piles, gravel beds	Worms, crickets, maggots, nightcrawlers
Bullhead	April thru Sept.	Lakes, ponds, and rivers	Shallow bays and weedy areas	Worms, crayfish, nightcrawlers, cutbaits
Carp	April thru Oct.	Lakes, ponds, and rivers	Grassy bays, stream channels	Prepared baits, worms, nightcrawlers
Crappie	Spring and fall, April thru Oct.	Lakes, rivers, and impoundments	Sunken brush, weed beds, deep holes, rip-rap, under-water structure	Minnows, jigs, spinners
Bass, Largemouth	Spring and fall, April thru Oct.	Lakes, rivers, and ponds	Weed beds, lily pads, submerged structure	Plastic worms, jigs, spinners, crankbaits, minnows, worms, crayfish
Bass, Smallmouth	Spring and fall, April thru Oct.	Lakes, rivers, and streams	Submerged structure, rip-rap, rocky areas, deep pools	Minnows, worms, crayfish, spinners, small crankbaits
Bass, Striped	Spring and fall, April thru Oct.	Lakes and impoundments	Submerged bars, rip-rap, spillways rocky areas, channels	Large minnows, spoons, spinners, crankbaits, jigs, crayfish
Bass, White	Spring and fall, April thru Oct.	Rivers and lakes	Rip-rap, tailwaters, dams, rocky areas, wing dams, points	Minnows, small spinners, small jigs

202

FISHING RECOMMENDATIONS

QUICK REFERENCE FISHING CHART

SPECIES	TIME OF YEAR	SUGGESTED WATERS	SUGGESTED LOCATIONS	SUGGESTED BAITS
Muskie	Spring and fall	Rivers and lakes	Weed lines, dropoffs, weed beds, submerged structure	Large minnows, jerkbaits, spoons, crankbaits, spinners
Pike, Northern	Spring and fall	Lakes and rivers	Weed beds, shallow bays, brush piles, sandbars	Large minnows, jerkbaits, spoons, crankbaits, spinners
Sunfish	April thru Oct.	Lakes, ponds, and rivers	Weed beds. gravel beds, brush piles	Crickets, worms, maggots, flies, wax worms
Walleye	Spring and fall	Lakes and rivers	Dropoffs, bars, rocky bottoms, submerged structure	Minnows, worms, jigs, crankbaits, spinners, spoons
Trout, Brown	Oct. thru May	Great Lakes, streams, and rivers	Offshore trolling, shoreline fishing deep holes, rip-rap, underwater structure	Spawn, flies, smelt, alewives, spoons, spinners, plugs
Trout, Rainbow (Steelheads)	Spring and fall	Great Lakes, rivers, and streams	Offshore trolling, shoreline fishing, deep holes, rip-rap, underwater structure	Spawn, flies, smelt, alewives, spoons, spinners, plugs
Salmon, Chinook	July thru Oct.	Great Lakes, rivers, and streams	Offshore trolling, shoreline fishing, deep holes, rip-rap, underwater structure	Spawn, flies, smelt, alewives, spoons, spinners, plugs
Salmon, Coho	Spring and fall	Great Lakes, rivers, and streams	Offshore trolling, shoreline fishing, deep holes, rip-rap, underwater structure	Spawn, flies, smelt, alewives, spoons, spinners, plugs, nightcrawlers
Perch	May thru Sept.	Great Lakes, rivers, and lakes	Submerged bars, rip-rap, rocky areas, channels, harbors	Jigs, spinners, minnows, worms, crayfish

203

BLUE GILL FISHING TIPS AND FACTS

BLUEGILL FACTS

COLOR IDENTIFICATION

The color of a bluegill can vary from lake to lake making it difficult to identify it from the many panfish found in most lakes. The most distinguishing things to look for in a bluegill is the black tab at the tip of the gill cover, a small gill cover, a small mouth, dark vertical stripes on the sides, and a dark spot at the bottom of the dorsal fin. If you find all of these, it's most likely a bluegill.

GROWTH

Bluegills spawn in the spring, laying as many as 38,000 eggs when the water temperature reaches 67 degrees. After the eggs hatch, the fry can grow as much as 4" during a single summer season, although this size is generally achieved in two to three years. Most bluegills mature to a respectable size of 6 to 7 inches in 8 years, but a really nice one can be 10 to 11 inches when fully grown.

BLUEGILL FISHING

WHEN AND WHERE TO LOOK FOR BLUEGILLS

The best time to fish for bluegills is during their spawning cycles. Down in the southern states, spawning takes place as early as February and continues periodically through August. In the northern and western states, spawning begins about mid-May and is completed in mid-September.

The best time to look for bluegill spawning beds is within five days of a full moon. For some unexplained reason, it's been observed by biologists and experienced bluegill fishermen that bluegills spawn most frequently around a full moon period.

When looking for spawning beds, look for sand or gravel bottomed areas with rocks, weeds, or other types of cover near by. The beds most often will be in two to four feet deep water, but occasionally can be found as deep as fourteen feet.

BLUEGILL GEAR

Matching the equipment to the conditions and size of the fish you're after is the key to enjoyable bluegill fishing.

Rod and reel selections usually consist of ultralite gear, such as short delicate rods from 4 feet in length to 20 foot noodle rods matched with tiny reels and equipped with light line in the two- to six-pound test class.

Some bluegill anglers prefer using superfine one-pound test line; however, the lighter the line the greater the potential you have of losing a slab-size bluegill.

Whatever equipment you select, it should be light and reliable, it doesn't have to be fancy to enjoy bluegill fishing.

CARP FISHING

If you're a carp fisherman, you probably know what a challenge it is to hook and land one of these bulldozers, and how many hours of fun you can have fishing for them.

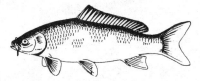

If you haven't tried carp fishing, you should just for the challenge or as a test of your fishing skills. After you do and you land a few big ones, you may give the carp a little more respect. Most carp are caught using dough bait concoctions, which are simple to prepare and easy to use. The following are just a few of the many recipes available for making dough baits that work.

DOUGH BAIT RECIPES

■ ■ ■ ■

- 1 cup of yellow cornmeal
- 2 heaping tablespoons of oatmeal
- 1 level teaspoon of sugar
- 1 cup of cold water

Combine ingredients and heat over a medium flame, stirring constantly for five to seven minutes or until the dough becomes a stiff ball.

Remove the mixture from the heat and add a half cup of dry cornmeal and mix it into the stiff ball. After it cools a little, knead the ball with your hands until the cornmeal is completely mixed into the ball.

■ ■ ■ ■

- 1 cup yellow cornmeal
- 1 cup flour
- 1 teaspoon sugar
- 1 quart of water
- 1 cup corn syrup

Mix the cornmeal, flour, and sugar with enough water to form a heavy dough, and make nickel-size balls out of it. Next, mix the quart of water with the syrup and bring it to a boil. Drop the balls into the boiling mixture for two to three minutes. The balls are done when they bounce when dropped on a hard surface.

■ ■ ■ ■

- 1 cup of flour
- 1 cup of cottonseed oil
- 1 cup of cereal (cornflakes, wheaties, or bran)
- 1 cup of oatmeal
- 1 cup of molasses
- 1 cup of water
- 1/4 cup of vanilla extract

Mix the cottonseed oil with the flour. Next, mix the cereal, oatmeal, molasses, vanilla, and water thoroughly. Add this mixture to the cottonseed/flour mixture and knead by hand until you achieve the proper texture.

■ ■ ■ ■

- 1 can (no.2) cream style corn
- 2 tablespoons of salt
- 1 cup of yellow cornmeal
- 1 cup of white flour
- 1 package of Sur-Gel
- 1 egg
- 1-1/2 cups of wheat germ

Heat the canned corn to a near boil and add the salt and cornmeal stirring until the mixture stiffens. Remove from the heat and place the mixture on a board or table and fold in the Sur-Gel, raw egg, and the wheat germ. Knead the mixture by hand until all the ingredients are thoroughly worked in.

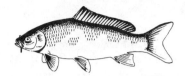

DOUGH BAIT RECIPES
(continued)
■ ■ ■ ■

- 2 cups of flour
- 3 cups of white cornmeal
- 1 cup of sugar
- 2 egg whites
- 1 cup of water
- 1 small box of anise seed

Mix ingredients together and stir to an even consistency until you have a stiff dough. Flatten the dough to a 1 to 1-1/2 inch thickness, wrap it in a cloth, and tie it up with a string. Place the cloth sack into a pot of boiling water for 6 minutes, moving the sack occasionally. Reduce the heat, and allow it to simmer for an additional 15 minutes. After it cools, work the dough thoroughly with your hands and re-wrap it in the cloth for storage.

■ ■ ■ ■

- 2 cups of cornmeal
- 3/4 cup of flour
- Water
- 1/2 small bottle of anise extract
- I box strawberry jello

Boil the jello in a pot per the instructions on the package, add the cornmeal and stir thoroughly. Remove from the heat, and add the anise extract and the flour and again mix thoroughly while it cools. As it cools, it will become the consistency of putty, at which time, pour it onto waxed paper or a shallow pan and allow it to cool until it eventually becomes hard. Refrigerate or freeze, until you're ready to use it.

■ ■ ■ ■

- 3 heaping cups of cornmeal
- 1-1/2 heaping cups of flour
- 1 pint of water
- 4 tablespoons of sugar
- 4 tablespoons of vanilla extract
- 2 teaspoons of anise seeds
- 2 packages of gelatin
  (Strawberry or blackberry)

In a bowl, mix the cornmeal and flour and set it aside. In a pot, mix the water, sugar, vanilla, and anise and bring it to a boil. Add the gelatin, which will foam up, and stir until the foam reaches the top of the pot. Remove the pot from the heat, and mix in the cornmeal and flour mixture. Stir with a heavy spoon until the mixture has the consistency of putty. Divide the dough into usable portions, wrapping them in waxpaper. Refrigerate the portions until you're ready to use them.

■ ■ ■ ■

- 1 box of bran flakes
- 3 ounces of grated longhorn cheese
- 5 tablesoons of honey
- Water as needed
- Flour as needed

Crush the bran flakes and add the cheese, honey, and water to make a doughy consistency using your hands. To stiffen up the mixture, use flour as needed.

■ ■ ■ ■

- 1/2 can of juice from canned corn
- 1/2 can of canned corn
- Cornmeal as needed
- Flour as needed

Blend corn and juice in blender and bring mixture to a boil in a pot. Add cornmeal until mass is solid. Remove from heat and knead in the flour until the right texture is achieved.

CRAPPIE FISHING TIPS AND FACTS

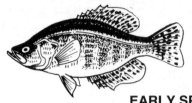

HABITAT
Black crappie prefer cool weedy waters with hard bottoms, while the white crappie favor the turbid waters of silty rivers and lakes with mud bottoms.

EARLY SPRING CRAPPIES
After the winter snow melts or a heavy spring rain, look under the brushy shorelines where high water has covered areas that are normally dry.

BASIC CRAPPIE JIGGING RIGS

The examples shown here are only a few of the many jigging rigs used for crappie fishing. The top rig consists of a feathered jig, while the center rig uses a curly tail. The bottom rig is an example of combining a feather jig with a live bait offering. All of these rigs can be worked over brush piles or any of the locations listed in the chart below.

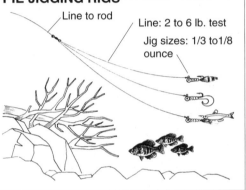

Line to rod

Line: 2 to 6 lb. test

Jig sizes: 1/3 to1/8 ounce

SEASONAL CRAPPIE LOCATIONS/PRESENTATIONS

Season	Locations	Presentation
Spring March thru April	3' to 15' Water Shallow bays, feeder creeks, channels, brush piles, stumps, logs	Jig and minnow rigs, spinners, bobber rigs
Summer July thru Sept.	3' to 20' Water Shallow weed beds, brush piles, stumps, logs, weedy bays, deep edges of weed beds	Jigs, spinners, small crankbaits, live bait rigs
Fall Oct. thru Nov.	3' to 30' Water Weed line dropoffs, rock piles, channel edges, deep brush piles or timber	Jig and minnow rigs, live bait rigs, bobber rigs
Winter Dec. thru Feb.	3' to 30' Water Dropoffs, rock piles, channel edges, deep brush piles or timber	Jig and minnow rigs, live bait rigs, bobber rigs

BASS FISHING TIPS AND FACTS

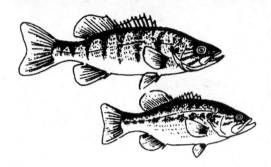

BEST BAIT

By far, the best proven bass bait is a juicy succulent night crawler or its counterpart, the plastic worm. The most successful rigging to use, is the Texas-style rig shown below. You can rig both a live crawler or one of the many plastic types using this technique.

TEXAS RIG

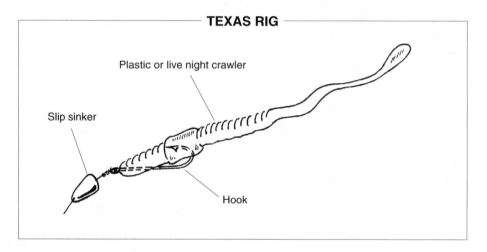

Plastic or live night crawler

Slip sinker

Hook

BASS FISHING/WATER TEMPERATURES

One of the key factors to successful bass fishing is water temperature. The following chart is a quick reference to improve your success.

WATER TEMPERATURE	FISH ACTIVITY	LURE TYPE PRESENTATION
Below 45 degrees	Very difficult to catch, sluggish, inactive	Live baits (Texas rig), small lures, jigs. Slow retreive.
Between 45 and 65 degrees	Moderately active	Live bait (Texas rig), buzz baits or spinner baits. Slow retreive, careful presentation.
Between 65 and 85 degrees	Most active	Live bait (Texas rig), buzz or spinner baits. Fast retreive.
Above 85 degrees	Inactive	Live baits (Texas rig), small lures, jigs. Slow retreive.

LARGEMOUTH BASS FISHING TIPS AND FACTS

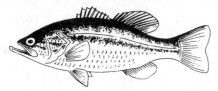

The following are a few general tips on fishing for largemouth bass.

BASS FACTS

■ Bass are most active at water temperatures of 60° to 75°.

■ Largemouths prefer shallower, warmer water than other types of bass do. They are most at home in weeds and other thick cover.

FISHING LILY PADS

When fishing for largemouths, it's important to approach the area to be fished as silently as possible. The slightest noise will spook largemouths, sending them off to deep water.

If shore fishing, walk softly; if boat fishing, use an electric motor or a push pole to get to the fishing area. Structure to a largemouth usually means lily pads. Largemouth bass and lily pads are synonymous.

The best pads will have a drop-off or channel leading to them, and will be in three or more feet of water. This type of bed will nearly always hold a number of bass.

To work the bed, cast a weedless spoons with a pork/frog/eel strip trailers into any of the holes in the middle of the pad and retrieve it right over the top, allowing it to flutter down as you go from hole to hole.

Another effective presentation is a weedless-rigged plastic worm. The plastic worm is one of the most versatile lures for pad fishing when rigged Texas-style. It is virtually weedless, allowing you the ability to reach some of the tough spots bass love to hide in.

When using plastic worms, have wide color selections such as blues, purples, grapes, motor oils, browns, oranges, chartreuse, reds, whites, and yellows. For clear water, use solid colors; for stained and muddy water, use metal flaked and fluorescent.

FISHING PIERS AND PILINGS

In addition to lily pads, other areas to try where largemouth bass concentrate are piers and bridges. They can be found in the channels under a bridge or under a pier or dock holding tight against the support pilings. Try putting your presentation as close as possible to the pilings for the best results.

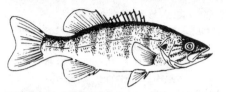

The following are a few general tips on fishing for smallmouth bass.

BASS FACTS

■ Smallmouth bass prefer deeper, clearer, cooler waters with rocky structure in streams, rivers and lakes.

■ Crayfish are the best live bait selection when fishing for smallmouths,

EARLY SEASON SMALLMOUTHS

Twister Tail Jigs

Try this rig for early season smallmouth. Use a one-eighth or one-quarter ounce leadhead jig with a 3-inch twister tail.

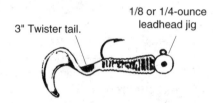

3" Twister tail.

1/8 or 1/4-ounce leadhead jig

Never use the same colored tail as the jighead. Contrast the color combinations such as a chartreuse jighead and a white or black tail, orange head with a yellow tail, or a white head with a gray tail. They may be strange color combinations, but you may get a surprise when they produce fish.

Single Blade Spinnerbaits

Another thing to try during early season smallmouth fishing is spinnerbaits. The right type and size are crucial during this time for success. Use smaller one-quarter-ounce, single-spin baits. The blade should be nickel in clear water and brass or copper in stained water. The most effective skirt colors are white, yellow, or chartreuse.

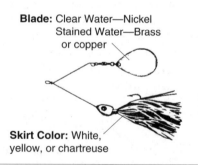

Blade: Clear Water—Nickel
Stained Water—Brass
or copper

Skirt Color: White, yellow, or chartreuse

STREAM AND RIVER TIPS

When selecting a stream or river for smallmouth fishing, certain general physical characteristics should be noted. This is especially important when both trout and smallmouths are resident. Look for the following conditions:

1. Clear water: Smallmouths cannot tolerate murky, silty, or muddy water.

2. Rocky or gravel bottoms: Smallmouths prefer rocky areas, especially around boulders or rock piles.

3. Water temperature: Smallmouths prefer water temperatures ranging from 55° to 70° F. Spawning temperatures range from 60° to 65° F and in some areas as high as 70°. Feeding shuts down when the temperature is below 50° or above 70° F.

FISHING STREAM AND RIVER BACKWATERS

A good location to try when river or stream fishing for smallmouths is at the head of a weed bed with a decent current flow around it.

The current forms a bar in front of the bed, which is a favorite spot for the smallmouth to set up housekeeping. These small bars, where the current splits and forms an area of reduced flow along the sides of the bed, are an excellent feeding source. In most cases, the fish will be located at the front of the bed. You may also find them at the back of the weed bed as shown in the following diagram.

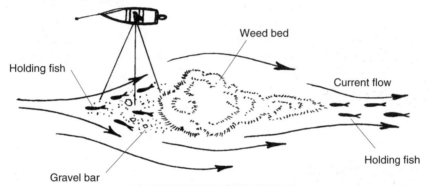

Holding fish

Weed bed

Current flow

Holding fish

Gravel bar

CONVERGING CHANNELS

Another good location will be an area where two channels converge (see the following diagram). The channels will create bars and weed flats, producing good feeding areas. The larger the weed flats bordering the channels are, the better the fishing.

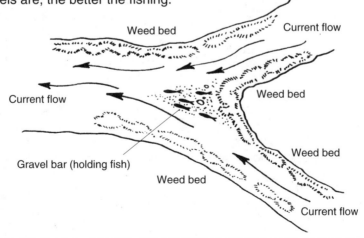

Weed bed

Current flow

Current flow

Weed bed

Gravel bar (holding fish)

Weed bed

Weed bed

Current flow

WHITE BASS FACTS

The white bass range has been artificially extended by transplanting throughout a wide area of the United States. It is considered the only bass found exclusively in fresh water. It is found in large streams, rivers, and lakes, and a typical adult will run about a pound or two, with some adults reaching a weight of three to four pounds.

There's an old saying, "When the lilacs are in bloom, the white bass are spawning." Lilacs don't trigger the spawning; the water temperature does. White bass spawn from late April to early June depending on their geographic location. Spawning occurs once every three or four years when the water temperature ranges from 58 to 64 degrees.

A mature female will lay between a half million to a million eggs in clean graveled nesting areas with the eggs hatching within 24 to 48 hours. The young fish form large schools and within a week's time begin their lives as predators leaving the nesting areas in search for food.

The life expectancy of the white bass in northern waters is approximately four to five years with a few reaching the age of nine years in cooler waters.

FALL FISHING FOR WHITE BASS

Equipment:

Rods: Ultralite spinning rod, 4-1/2 to 5 feet, somewhat on the "stiff" side, and a 7-foot spinning stick rigged with a slip bobber.

Reels: Spinning filled to within 1/8" of the lip of the spool.

Line: 4 lb. test on the ultralite, and 6 lb. test on the spinning stick.

Lures: Wide variety of small spoons or spinners that can be trolled or cast, and leadhead jigs in the 1/32, 1/16, and 1/8 oz. sizes.

Baits: Leeches, minnows, and 2-inch shiners.

Technique: To locate fish, drift fish with a minimum of line out working 7- to 15-foot depths using baited jigs so they ride along just over the bottom.

Occasionally raise the rod straight up as you move along, allowing it slowly down while keeping the slack out.

After a strike, as you catch your first fish, mark the location with a marker buoy. After landing the fish, anchor within casting range of the marker and cast out the slip bobber rig set at a 7-foot depth.

Using the ultralite rig, start working the area by fan casting and bottom bouncing until you locate the main concentration of fish.

If you get a hit on the slip bobber rig, you know the fish are suspended, at which time you should adjust your retrieve on the ultralite. Otherwise, increase the depth of the slip bobber rig if you start catching fish on the ultralite.

MUSKIE FISHING TIPS AND FACTS

MUSKIE FACTS

DIET

Muskie eat most any kind of fish, including their own species. They also will eat frogs, muskrats, squirrels, beavers, mice, ducks, ducklings, birds, and sometimes snakes.

ELUSIVE MUSKIE

It takes an estimated average of 700-man hours for each muskie caught by hook and line.

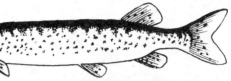

MUSKIE FISHING

BEST MUSKIE WATERS

The following list of locations are considered the best areas to fish for muskie in both Canada and the United States.

CANADA:
Ontario-Vermilion Bay Area,
Fort Francis Area,
Lake of the Woods, Kenora Area
Quebec- St. Lawrence River drainage

UNITED STATES:
Minnesota-Lake of the Woods,
Leech Lake, Cass Lake
Wisconsin-Eagle River Area,
Hayward Area, Chipewa Flowage
New York-Lake Chautauqua,
St. Lawrence River
Michigan-Lake St. Clair,
St. Clair River
Pennsylvania-Allegheny River,
French Creek
Ohio-Muskingum River
West Virginia-Elk River
Kentucky-Obed River
Tennessee-Crab Orchard Creek

LURE SPEED

Many muskie guides claim that a slow moving lure or retrieve will catch more big ones more often than a fast retrieve.

LURE SELECTION CHART

The following chart offers suggestions on the type of lures to use under various weather and water conditions.

Weather/Water Conditions	Lure Choice
Flat calm, weedy,	
Clear water	1, 2, 3, 4
Dark water	1, 2, 3,
Flat calm, deep weeds/cover	
Clear water	1, 2, 3, 4
Dark water	1, 2, 3
Breezy, high wave action, weedy,	
Clear water	1, 2
Dark water	1, 2
Breezy, high wave action, deep weeds/cover	
Clear water	1, 2
Dark water	1, 2

Lure Legend
1. Buzz baits/spinners-Northland Buzzard, Mepps Giant Killer
2. Floating propeller baits-Pfluger Globe, Cisco Kid topper
3. Crawler type baits-muskie jitterbug, crazy crawler, Doc's Creeper, Hawg wobblers
4. Top water baits- Heddon Flaptail, Rapala Magnum

NORTHERN PIKE FACTS

MOST ACTIVE

Northerns are the most active during the mid-morning hours and the midafternoon hours. Generally they don't feed at night.

TOOTH LOSS

Northerns don't loose their teeth during the hot summer months as the old saying goes. They may loose a few on turtles or artificial lures, but not because of the weather.

During the hot sizzling summer months, fish deeper waters to be more successful.

HABITAT

Large pike can be caught when you concentrate your efforts in lakes that are capable of producing them.

Such lakes have environmental conditions which allow pike to reach their growth potential of 25 pounds plus. These lakes have an abundance of food, shallow areas with adequate weed cover for spawning purposes and deep water which provide cover after they mature.

The lake can be a medium size (930 acres) or a large body of water such as reservoir or impoundment. Large pike are adaptable to both shallow or deep waters. They prefer deep water; however, if they can't satisfy their hunger they will make short forays to the shallows in search for food and to spawn during the spring spawning season.

The major food of the large pike is other fish. They prefer live ones; however, they are also known to be scavengers that will eat dead fish. When pike fry hatch, they don't consume any food during the first five days. They are nourished by a yolk sac attached to their stomach. After the fifth day, they feed on small minnows and tiny aquatic organisms, at which time they spread out in search of food to grow to their potential 25 pounds or more.

LOCATING/CATCHING PIKE

The key to catching large pike is deep water. However, fish behavior is as predictable as the weather, so you never know, you may be at the right spot, deep or shallow, and end up with a wall hanger.

Northern pike are especially fond of lurking around weed beds. Check out any submerged weed beds in 10 to 15 feet of water with deeper waters close by. Northerns often lay in the deeper waters and move into the weed bed areas to feed. Work the weed beds with spoons, spinners, or jerk baits, or try using the live bait rig shown on the next page and one of their preferred baits.

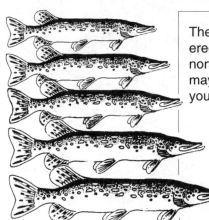

LIVE BAIT SELECTION-SIZE

The following information should be considered when using live baits when fishing for northern pike. The size of the bait you use may possibly determine the size northern you may catch.

Bait Size	Northern Pike Size
4" Bait	All sizes under 5 lbs. or less
6" Bait	3 to 8 lb. pike
8" Bait	5 to 15 lb. pike
12" Bait	Over 8 lb. pike
Baits over 12"	Lunker pike 15 lbs. or over

BAIT PREFERENCE-MINNOWS

The following are the preferred baits (minnows) of the northern pike.

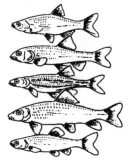

1. Shiners-medium size
2. Creek chubs (redtail)-medium size
3. Dace minnows-large size
4. Suckers-very small
5. Fathead minnows-very large

BEST LIVE BAIT RIG

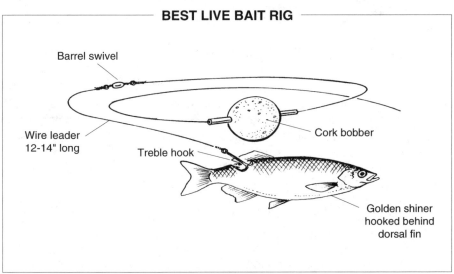

Barrel swivel

Wire leader
12-14" long

Treble hook

Cork bobber

Golden shiner
hooked behind
dorsal fin

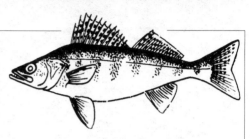

WALLEYE FACTS
HABITAT

Walleye are open water fish that prefer deep water. Following their instincts, they shun shallow, weedy shorelines when searching for food.

Walleye will sometimes rise to a high running lure, but normally they are bottom feeders in deep water. Fish them close to the bottom in deep water.

WHITE EYES

Because of the lack of pigmentation, the eyes of a walleye are very sensitive to light. On bright days, fish deep for better results.

FISHING FOR WALLEYES
USING JIGS

Walleyes for the most part are very color conscious. The following is a rule of thumb for selecting color and jig sizes that have proven to be very productive based on the percentage of the times they are used.

Preferred Jig Color Selection							
Color	Orange	Yellow	Chartreuse	Pink	Green	Purple	Blue
Percentage Used	30%	20%	20%	20%	10%	10%	10%

Preferred Jig Sizes to use				
Size (ounces)	1/32 oz.	1/16 oz.	1/8 oz.	1/4 oz
Percentage Used	20%	25%	25%	5%

Preferred Retrieve

The following is a common retrieve to use when using jigs dressed with crawlers or minnows. Different actions can be obtained by changing the jig head size or varying the speed of the retrieve. Each jig will respond differently to your rod action depending on its size. Tiny 1/32 to 1/16 ounce jigs respond gently in a waving action or a soft swim, while 1/8 or 1/4 ounce jigs respond with a sharp well-defined jerk. However, both types are used with the following retrieve.

Make your cast, then point the rod tip toward the bait (rod tip close to the water). Using the rod tip, pull the jig-head toward you in a series of small (4 to 6 inch) jerks. Lower the rod tip and reel in the slack line and repeat the small rod tip jerks again. Keep repeating until you're done reeling in your line.

FISHING FOR WALLEYE

SPRING WALLEYE

Spring ushers in the spawning season for the walleye. Spawning takes place when the water temperature reaches 45° to 50° F. During the spring, walleyes move into the shallows. Fish gravel or rocky areas in shallower waters using light gear.

FALL WALLEYE

Fall walleye are hungry and aggressive; use large minnows—redtails 3 to 6 inches or big shiners.

SUMMER WALLEYE

During the summer months fish deep water structure. Best results are obtained during early morning, late evening, or at night.

WINTER WALLEYE

During the winter, movement patterns and feeding habits of the walleye slow down. Walleye feed once every three days during the winter months.

WALLEYE NIGHT FISHING

The following are a few tips on night fishing for walleye.

■ Check out the area you plan to fish during daylight. Locate structure, snags, and so forth.

■ Mark the spots to be fished with buoy markers during daylight.

■ If trolling, plan your passes during daylight. Set the depths you plan to troll after dark.

■ Organize your boat, tacklebox, and equipment prior to going out.

■ Take along some good lighting (flashlight, headlamp, lantern).

■ Try fluorescent or lighted floats for still fishing.

■ Try fluorescent lures or jigs, or add a piece of reflective tape to your favorite lures.

WALLEYE RIVER FISHING RIG

Tie on a 1/4 oz. bright orange marabou jig (size 2.0 or 3.0 hook) in place of the sinker used on a typical 15-inch leader river rig. Next, tie on the dropper line (24-inch leader) with a 3- to 4-inch-long orange or red marabou streamer fly.

Cast the rig upstream, allowing it to settle on the bottom, and then work it back through the eddies, making sure it bounces along the bottom during the retrieve.

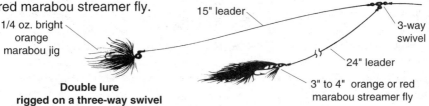

15" leader

1/4 oz. bright orange marabou jig

3-way swivel

24" leader

3" to 4" orange or red marabou streamer fly

**Double lure
rigged on a three-way swivel**

TROUT FISHING TIPS AND FACTS

LOCATING TROUT

Look for splashy water around sunken boulders or rapids. You can also find them where there is beaver activity.

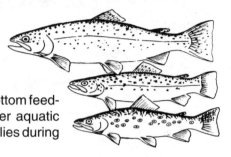

SPRING TROUT

Early lethargic spring trout prefer bottom feeding where insect nymphs and other aquatic foods are abundant. Use weighted flies during this period, fishing on the bottom.

USING LEECHES

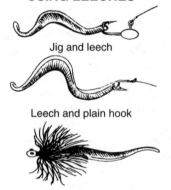

Jig and leech

Leech and plain hook

Marabou jig and leech

Here's a presentation that will produce trout, and large ones. It consists of working a jig tipped with a leech along the undercuts along the banks of your favorite trout stream.

While it will work with a plain hook, you will take more fish if you use a marabou jig along with the leech. The marabou jig in combination with the leech will add the action necessary to trigger a large trout into biting.

As far as the marabou jig color is concerned, stay with the natural colors, brown or black. Hook the leech below the sucker behind the jig and start fishing. If fished properly, you have a combination which will be hard for a large trout to avoid.

USING MINNOWS

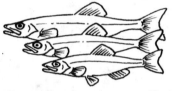

The larger the trout, the more likely his diet consists of minnows, chubs, and other small fish 3 to 4 inches long. With that in mind, here's a presentation utilizing its favorite food.

Using a long shank Aberdeen hook, run the hook through the minnow's mouth and out the gill cover. Then place the barb of the hook into the side of the minnow making your presentation virtually snagless.

Using only enough weight to keep the minnow flowing naturally with the current, work the presentation along the bank undercuts and deep holes of your favorite trout stream.

Since trout almost entirely face the direction of the current waiting for food, you can also cast upstream allowing the minnow to be carried downstream by the current, making it visible to the trout for the longest possible time. Keep a tight line, and when a strike is felt, set the hook immediately because a trout hits hard and fast.

SALMON FISHING TIPS AND FACTS

SALMON FACTS

Salmon can be found from the Pacific coast and the upper east coast of the United States as well as the Great Lakes region. Salmon in general spend their entire adult lives in saltwater and spawn in fresh water after they mature to adulthood.

In the Great Lakes region, various salmon species were introduced by conservation groups as an experiment to improve sport fishing. The experiment was a success, with the various species adapting to a freshwater environment where they spend their entire lives. These freshwater species spawn starting in late September through November, providing some of the best sport fishing found anywhere.

SALMON FISHING

With the introduction of the salmon into the Great Lakes, sport fishing has become a very popular sport. Great Lakes salmon can be caught stream fishing, shore fishing, or boat fishing using spinning gear, bait casting equipment, or fly fishing.

During most of the open water season, charter boat fishing is available to the sportsman from most boat harbors for a nominal fee. Fishing from the shore or one of the many piers found along the lake also provides excellent fishing.

The following is a general list of basic equipment that can be used for shore or pier fishing in the Great Lakes region for salmon.

TACKLE SUGGESTIONS FOR SHORE OR PIER FISHING

- Three heavy duty rods and reels (two to use, one as a spare)
- Reels filled to capacity (300 yards) of 12 to 15 lb. test line
- Assorted lures: Silver/blue/green 3-1 1/2 ounce and 2-3/4 ounce, Mr. Champs, Cleo's, assorted jigs, large streamer flies, and so forth
- Assorted snap swivels
- Two dozen assorted size sinkers: Split shots, egg, dipsey
- Two dozen #2/0, long shank hooks or floating jig heads
- Minnow bucket

- Stringer with a 20 ft. cord
- Assorted bait: Alewives, large minnows, spawn sacks, pork rind, marshmallows, whole kernel canned corn
- Landing net with extendable handle (10 ft. or more)
- 5-gallon carry-all pail or bucket
- Fishing license with a trout/salmon stamp
- Tackle box for extra equipment
- Extra warm clothing (just in case the weather changes)

PERCH FISHING TIPS AND FACTS

PERCH FACTS

■ ■ ■ ■

Perch spawn when the water temperature ranges from 45° to 50° F. They are most active when the water temperature is in the range of 55° to 70° F.

Female perch grow larger than males, attaining lengths of 13" to 15" or larger, while the male seldom exceeds 12". Anything over 12" is considered a jumbo perch.

■ ■ ■ ■

Perch school by size (the larger the fish, the smaller the school), and the schools travel next to each other when they are searching for food. The larger jumbo perch stay segregated from the smaller perch because the smaller perch are quicker, making it difficult for the larger slower jumbos to compete for the food.

■ ■ ■ ■

When you're catching small perch, try moving your offering a few yards in various directions until you find the jumbos which may be only a few yards away.

PERCH FISHING

Perch fishing is synonymous with the Great Lakes region of the United States. However, they are also found throughout many lakes, rivers, and streams, making them one of the most frequently sought species of fish by many anglers.

TACKLE SUGGESTIONS FOR GREAT LAKES PERCH FISHING

- Two ultralight rods and reels
- Reels filled to capacity with 4 lb. test line
- Minnow bucket with at least 4 dozen small perch minnows
- Two dozen crayfish (crabs)
- Landing net with a 10-foot handle
- Two dozen #10 short shanked hooks
- Two dozen B-B split shot sinkers (assorted sizes)
- Stringer with a 20 ft. cord
- 5-gallon carry all pail or bucket
- Fishing license
- Small box for extra tackle (hooks, line, sinkers, and so forth)
- Extra warm clothing (just in case the weather changes)

■ ■ ■ ■
BEST BAITS

When the water temperature is below 55° F, use minnows or shiners. When the water temperature exceeds 55° F, use crayfish (softshells).

Another bait to use during summer fishing are maggots, which at times will produce excellent results.

■ ■ ■ ■
BEST TIME

Under favorable conditions, perch are active from dawn till about 8:00 A.M., and again from 11:00 A. M. to about 2:00 P.M., and also about two hours before sunset.

CATFISH FACTS

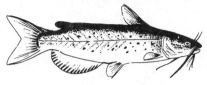

Catfish feed most actively when the water temperature is between 65° to 85° F. The best temperature is from 75° to 80°, which increases their metabolic rate to its maximum.

HABITAT

Channel cats prefer moving water, while flatheads stay where the water is quiet.

CATFISH FISHING

Standard equipment for catfishing consists of a pole with plenty of backbone, 15 to 25 lb. test line, a single no. 2 or no. 4 hook tied to a 3- to 6-foot leader attached to a barrel swivel with a sliding sinker above it.

The hook can be baited with any number of concoctions such as blood baits, stink baits, leeches, worms, chicken entrails, hotdogs, or small fish like bluegills, shad, chubs, or suckers.

To improve your ability to catch catfish, try either early morning fishing from just before daybreak or from dusk to midnight or later.

FISHING TIP

To get the catfish in a feeding mood, fill a quart-size milk carton with chicken or beef liver blood and punch some holes in the carton. Then suspend it over a good catfish hole and wait about 15 minutes before fishing. Fish a few feet from the carton for the best results.

BULLHEAD FACTS

Bullheads probably are caught by more young neophyte anglers than any other species of fish.

Almost anyone can find bullheads within a short distance from their home in nearby ponds, rivers, streams, or lakes.

Bullheads are active from May through October with the peak fishing season being in the months of July through September.

They are active during evening hours feeding primarily on insects .

HABITAT

Bullheads prefer sluggish waters with weedy bottoms and are cover-oriented. They like rocks, sunken logs, and brush piles.

BULLHEAD FISHING

Medium action equipment rigged with 6 to 8 lb. test line and a no. 6 hook works the best. Sinkers (like a few split shots) can be used for stream or river fishing; however, don't use any when fishing lakes or ponds.

The hooks can be baited with nightcrawlers, leaf worms , small minnows, or hotdogs, which will produce good results.

BULLHEAD BAIT TIP

Here's a tip I got from a young boy fishing at a local pond. If you want to catch bullheads, use lima beans! Bullheads seem to love canned lima beans better than worms or most other baits. At least they do in our local pond.

STRIPED BASS FACTS

Back in 1941, a new freshwater fishery was created in South Carolina when the Santee River was dammed, trapping saltwater stripers in Lake Marion.

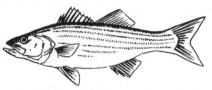

The stripers survived the water change and thrived in the new impoundment and began spawning. Since then, in the United States, twenty-seven states have introduced striped bass in various large lakes, rivers, and impoundments. The following is a list of the states where striped bass were introduced:

Alabama, Arizona, Arkansas, California, Florida, Georgia, Illinois, Indiana, Iowa, Kansas, Kentucky, Louisiana, Mississippi, Missouri, Nebraska, Nevada, New Mexico, North Carolina, Ohio, Oklahoma, Pennsylvania, South Carolina, Tennessee, Texas, Utah, Virginia, and West Virginia.

STRIPED BASS FISHING

Striped bass behavior and feeding habits are similar to the crappie. For the most part, techniques used for crappie fishing will also work when fishing for stripers. The only differences are the size of the baits you use and the type of equipment.

The baits will be larger and the tackle will be heavier. Trolling, jigging, or casting are some of the more effective methods to use, using live baits as well as artificials. The following chart shows some of the most popular effective striper baits to use.

Bait	Type	Season
Large gizzard shad	Live	All Seasons
Bluegills	Live	All Seasons
Large chubs	Live	All Seasons
Baltic minnow and jig with snatrix water snake (white)	Plug, jig combo	All Seasons
Bucktail jig (white)	Jig	Fall, Winter, Spring
White and yellow jigs	Jig	Summer, Winter
Norman's striper rig	Plug, jig combo	Summer, Winter
Rogue (bone)	Plug	Spring
Redfin (bone or chrome)	Plug	Spring
Rapalas	Plug	Fall, Winter, Spring
Little "N" (bone)	Plug	Fall, Spring
Hellbender	Plug	Summer, Winter
Rebels	Plug	Summer, Winter
Mann-O-Lure	Spoon	Summer